BLUE-RIBBON PICKLES & PRESERVES

Also by Maria Polushkin Robbins

The Cook's Quotation Book

The Dumpling Cookbook

Blue-Ribbon Pies

PICKLES & PRESERVES

EDITED BY

MARIA POLUSHKIN ROBBINS

ST. MARTIN'S PRESS
NEW YORK

I would like to thank the Anchorage Fur Rendezvous, the Los Angeles County Fair, the State Fair of Oklahoma, the State Fair of Texas, and the Michigan 4-H Foundation for allowing me to reprint recipes from cookbooks they have published.

Design by Claire B. Counihan

Library of Congress Cataloging-in-Publication Data

Robbins, Maria Polushkin.
Blue-ribbon pickles and preserves.

1. Pickles 2. Cookery (Relishes) 3. Cookery (Jam) 4. Canning and preserving. I. Title.
TX805.P65 1987 641.4'6 87-1698
ISBN 0-312-00733-7

First Edition
10 9 8 7 6 5 4 3 2 1

Contents

Pickles & Relishes

PRESERVES
Including Jams, Conserves, Jellies, Butters, and Chutneys

Preserves (*cont.*)

Acknowledgments

This book would not have happened without tons of generous help from the officers of the state and regional fair organizations, who waded through their records to send me the names and addresses of their prizewinning cooks, and, of course, most of all from the cooks themselves, who shared their recipes with me and readers of this book. My heartfelt thanks to them all. Thanks, too, to Barbara Anderson, my editor, who was patient and helpful; Joan Whitman, my copy editor, who makes work seem more like play: and finally to my husband, Ken, who helped stuff and seal all those envelopes.

BLUE-RIBBON PICKLES & PRESERVES

Introduction

For many people, homemade condiments—pickles, relishes, preserves, jams, jellies, chutneys, fruit butters, and the like—represent little more than a dim, if quaint and pleasant, memory of hand-labeled mason jars neatly lined up in grandmother's pantry or snugged into a gift basket at Christmas. That's not surprising, given the hurried pace of modern life and the burgeoning availability of store-bought specialty food items, especially in our cities. Yet the appeal of "put up" foods remains intact, and in every part of the country there are people who take the time to preserve, not only the year's bumper crop of apples or zucchini, but the ancient and honorable (not to mention thrifty and delicious) art of putting things by.

If "thrifty" and "delicious" are not tempting enough, there is the luxury of knowing just *exactly* what has gone into your pear butter. On a cold and snowy winter's day, what better way to recapture the smells and tastes of summer than to uncap and consume a jar of raspberry jam with your muffins and tea? And with raspberry jam on your mind, what better excuse to go wandering through the fields in summer, even if half the day's gleanings are gone before you return home?

There are dozens of preservable foods growing in the fields and woods and gardens of America. For every one there are surely dozens of methods of preserving, and for each method surely a dozen variations. Yet for all that, I dare say there's not a variety that hasn't been entered in one or more of America's state or regional fairs. That enduring institution, the country fair, is the greatest repository of domestic craft and pride in the nation, and so it seemed natural to turn to that homey resource for a survey of all things pickled and preserved.

Tips for Making Perfect Pickles & Preserves

Basic Rules for Making Pickles, Relishes, Jellies, Jams, Preserves, Conserves, Chutneys, and Fruit Butters

Though extremely satisfying, making pickles or preserves is not a spur-of-the-moment activity. It takes planning and a leisurely amount of time. Before you get started, read through the following pages to make sure you have the necessary equipment and to acquaint yourself with basic procedures.

If you would like to have more detailed information about making pickles and preserves, the following publications are excellent:

Ball Blue Book, 30th Edition
Ball Corporation
Box 2005, Dept. PK 6A
Muncie, Indiana 47302

The New Putting Food By, published by The Stephen Greene Press

Equipment for Making Pickles and Preserves

- *Canning jars:* For best and safest results use canning jars with their appropriate lids. Mason, Kerr, or Ball jars come with two-piece vacuum lids. The dome lids and the screwbands are also sold separately. The jars and screwbands may be reused. The dome lids *cannot* be reused. Canning jars and lids may be purchased at hardware and kitchen supply stores. Do plan ahead and buy your jars before the canning season. *Do not* use jars leftover from another use, such as old mayonnaise or peanut butter jars. They will not stand up to heat processing and they cannot be vacuum sealed. Please read and follow the manufacturer's instructions for sealing the canning jars.

- *Preserving kettle:* Use a large, 8- to 10-quart kettle or pot with a flat, broad bottom for preparing fruits or vegetables. Stainless steel or enameled cast iron are best. The kettle must be big enough for the contents to come to a full, rolling boil without boiling over. The safest way is to make sure that the pot is never more than one-third full.
- *Water-bath canner:* This is a large enamelware pot fitted out with basketlike racks to hold the canning jars, keeping them from touching one another and permitting you to lift the jars out of the boiling water when they have been processed the proper amount of time. It must be deep enough for the water to cover the tops of the jars by 2 inches. Available in hardware stores and houseware departments, it is inexpensive.
- Another large pot in which to sterilize the canning jars, and a small saucepan in which to boil the lids.
- A candy/jelly thermometer—a special thermometer that records temperatures up to 400°F.
- Stoneware or pottery crocks, or deep stainless steel bowls for brining vegetables for pickles.
- Large colanders and strainers, made from plastic, enamel, or stainless steel. Do not use galvanized aluminum.
- A jelly bag for extracting juices from fruit. Jelly bags are available in houseware departments and by mail order. Several layers of closely woven cheesecloth may be used to line a colander as an improvised jelly bag.
- A jar-lifter, which is a special pair of tongs with rubberized clamps that enables you to lift hot jars out of boiling water.
- Kitchen scales.
- A food processor, meat grinder, or food chopper.

- Long-handled wooden spoons for stirring.
- A long-handled metal spoon for skimming, or a special long-handled skimmer.
- A wide-mouth funnel for pouring hot preserves into canning jars.
- A ladle to lift hot foods from the kettle into the funnel. A ladle with a spout is particularly useful.
- A clock with a large second hand for timing jellies and jams made with added pectin.
- Measuring cups and spoons.
- Plenty of pot holders and dish towels.

How to Proceed

1. Read through the recipe so that you know what you will be doing.
2. Assemble all necessary ingredients.
3. Assemble all necessary equipment.
4. Check canning jars for nicks or cracks. Pay particular attention to the surface along the top rim. Discard any that have irregularities—they will no longer be able to form a proper seal with the dome lid. Make sure you have enough new lids and enough screwbands to seal each jar.
5. *Sterilize jars and lids:* Wash all canning jars and lids in warm soapy water. Place jars in a large pot, cover with water, and bring to a boil. Boil for 15 minutes to sterilize. Place lids and screwbands in a smaller saucepan. Bring to a boil and boil for 15 minutes to sterilize. Leave jars and lids in hot water until ready to fill.
6. Prepare the fruit or vegetables as directed in the recipe.
7. *Making jelly:* If you are making jelly and extracting juice from prepared fruit, remember that it may take several hours for the juice to drip through the jelly bag. Do not attempt to hurry the process by squeezing the bag—this

will produce cloudy jelly. When the juice has dripped through, measure it; if there is not enough juice, pour a little water through the pulp in the jelly bag until you have the required amount. Wash, rinse, and dry the jelly bag carefully after each use.

8. *Using commercial pectin:* Follow directions carefully. When using pectin, it is important that the mixture boils as hard and as long as directed. Full, rolling boil means a boil that bubbles all across the surface of the mixture and cannot be stirred down. Start timing the boil when it reaches that point and boil for the exact amount of time indicated. Do not use a pot that is too small—the hot boiling mixture will boil over and you will have a horrible mess. If you are making jelly with added pectin, it will be properly done if you follow the directions in the individual recipe or in the instructions that come with the pectin.
9. *The jelly test:* For jellies made without added pectin you will need to test either with a thermometer or with a spoon. Jelly without added pectin is done when the temperature reaches 8°F above boiling. At sea level this is 220°F. If you do not have a thermometer, you can determine the jelling point by performing a sheeting test with a metal spoon. Dip a cold, dry, metal spoon into the boiling jelly. Hold it out of the steam and let it cool about 1 minute. Turn it sideways to watch the liquid run off. If the liquid runs together and falls off the spoon in a sheet, the jelly is done. If the drops remain separate the jelly is not yet done. Wash, dry, and cool the spoon in between tests.
10. *Skimming and stirring:* Remove the boiling mixture from the heat and skim the surface with a metal spoon or skimmer to remove any foam

that has formed on the surface. Preserves with whole pieces of fruit should be stirred carefully for 5 minutes or so to cool and prevent pieces of fruit from floating.

11. Remove sterilized jars and two-piece lids from hot water. Drain on toweling. Always pour hot ingredients into *hot* jars.
12. *Allow head room:* Ladle the hot mixture into hot sterilized jars. Each recipe will indicate the amount of headroom to leave. Headroom is the air space between the lids and the contents of the jar. This air space creates suction to ensure a perfect vacuum.
13. Seal the jars with two-piece lids following the manufacturer's instructions.
14. *Processing jars in boiling-water bath:* Pickles, relishes, jams, preserves, marmalade, butters, conserves, and chutneys should be processed in a boiling-water bath for the time indicated in the recipe. Only jellies are not processed in a boiling-water bath because it would make them cloudy. Set jars in racks of water-bath canner. Add boiling water to cover tops of jars by at least 2 inches. Bring the water-bath canner to a full boil over high heat and start timing. Add 1 minute more of boiling time for each 1,000 feet of elevation above sea level. When processing time has been completed, remove the jars to a towel-covered surface to cool. Do not place hot jars directly on a cold hard surface as they may crack.
15. *Checking the seal:* Let jars rest for 12 to 24 hours. Then check to see if seals are complete. With the two-piece vacuum lids, the center of the dome lid will be slightly depressed if the seal is complete. If it is still elevated, press it down gently. If it stays down, the seal is fine. If you have any doubts about the completeness

of the seal, refrigerate the product and use it as you would any other refrigerated food. Refrigerate and use any jam or jelly that is left over after filling the jars.

16. *Storing Pickles and Preserves:* Wipe the jars clean of any spills before storing. Label each jar with name and date, including the year. This will enable you to use the oldest jars first. Store in a cool, dark (away from sunlight) place. Most pickles, relishes, and chutneys will taste better if they are allowed to mellow and rest for 4 to 6 weeks before using.

A Few Words About Ingredients

- *Salt:* For best pickling results use pure salt without any additives. Most supermarkets sell canning/pickling salt in 5-pound bags, which is ideal. Do not use table salt as it is often iodized and has additives to keep it running in damp weather.
- *Vinegar:* Use a good quality white distilled vinegar or cider vinegar with 5 to 6 percent acidity. Do not use fancy flavored vinegars. Save them for salads.
- *Lime and alum:* Some old-time recipes call for the use of either alum or lime (calcium hydroxide or calcium hydrochloride). Both were used to make pickles crisper. Today it is felt that these additives are both unnecessary and possibly dangerous to health. None of the recipes used in this book requires the use of either lime or alum. Where they have been called for in the original recipe, I have listed them as optional ingredients.
- *Sugar:* Unless otherwise specified, use pure white granulated sugar. Brown sugar will affect the color of the pickles or preserves. Measure all ingredients according to recipe. Do not decrease amount of sugar or substitute artificial sweeteners as this will affect the jelling factor.
- *Pectin:* Commercial pectin comes in either liquid or powder form. They are *not* interchangeable. Use the type of pectin called for in each recipe.

PICKLES & RELISHES

Crab Apple Pickles

2 quarts crab apples with stems (about 2½ pounds)
2 cinnamon sticks
1½ tablespoons whole allspice
1½ tablespoons whole cloves
6 cups sugar
3 cups water
3 cups white vinegar
Red food coloring (optional)

Wash and remove blossom end of each apple—do not remove stems. To prevent apples from bursting when heated, prick each apple with a needle in four or five places. Tie spices in a cheesecloth bag. Combine sugar, water, and vinegar in a large pot. Add spice bag and red food coloring, if desired, and boil 5 minutes. Add crab apples to make a single layer and cook over medium heat until apples are almost tender. Carefully remove apples to a baking dish or bowl. Repeat until all apples are cooked. Pour boiling syrup over apples. Cover and refrigerate overnight (12 to 18 hours).

Sterilize canning jars and lids according to directions on page 5. Pack apples loosely into hot, sterile jars. Heat syrup to boiling and pour over apples, leaving ½-inch headspace. Seal with sterilized lids according to manufacturer's instructions. Process in a boiling-water bath for 15 minutes.

YIELD: About 5 pints.

Judi Roberts
Claremont,
California
Los Angeles
County Fair

Dilly Beans

2 pounds trimmed green beans
1 teaspoon cayenne pepper
4 garlic cloves
4 sprigs fresh dill
¼ cup pickling salt
2½ cups white vinegar
2½ cups water

Sterilize canning jars and lids according to directions on page 5.

Pack beans lengthwise into hot, sterile pint jars. To each jar add ¼ teaspoon cayenne pepper, 1 garlic clove, and 1 sprig of dill. Combine salt, vinegar, and water in a saucepan and bring to a boil. Pour, boiling hot, over beans, leaving ¼-inch headspace. Seal with sterilized lids according to manufacturer's instructions. Process in a boiling-water bath for 10 minutes.

YIELD: 4 pints.

Barbara Carpenter
Milwaukee,
Wisconsin
Wisconsin
State Fair

Pickled Beets I

40 to 50 small whole beets
2 cups white vinegar
2 cups sugar

Sterilize canning jars and lids according to directions on page 5.

Trim greens off the beets but leave a 1-inch stem. Do not peel the beets, and leave all of the root. Wash beets and boil them in water to cover for 15 minutes. Drain. When cool enough to handle, trim off roots and stem and slip off skins. Pack beets into hot, sterile pint jars. The beets may be packed whole, sliced, or diced. In a saucepan, bring vinegar and sugar to a boil. Dilute with water to taste and return to a boil. Fill jars with boiling syrup, leaving ½-inch headspace. Seal with sterilized lids according to manufacturer's instructions. Process in a boiling-water bath for 30 minutes.

YIELD: 5 to 6 pints.

Barbara Carpenter
Milwaukee, Wisconsin
Wisconsin State Fair

Pickled Beets II

3 pounds beets
1 stick cinnamon
1 teaspoon allspice
6 whole cloves
1 pint white vinegar
½ cup water
½ cup sugar

Sterilize canning jars and lids according to directions on page 5.

Trim greens off the beets but leave a 1-inch stem. Do not peel the beets, and leave all of the root. Cook beets in boiling water until tender, about 15 minutes. When cool enough to handle, trim off roots and stem and slip off skins. Slice them if you wish. Tie spices in cheesecloth. Heat vinegar, water, sugar, and spices to boiling. Add the beets, whole or sliced, and boil 5 minutes. Remove spice bag. Pack beets into sterilized jars and fill jars with hot liquid, leaving ½-inch headroom. Seal with sterilized lids according to manufacturer's instructions. Process in a boiling-water bath for 30 minutes.

YIELD: About 3 pints.

Malinda Lifer
Lancaster, Ohio
Fairfield
County Fair

Bread-and-Butter Pickles I

Mr. Pestana writes that this is an old family recipe he has modified to his own taste by adding cayenne pepper and pickling spices.

4 quarts medium-size pickling cucumbers
6 medium-size white onions
1 green bell pepper
1 red bell pepper
3 garlic cloves
⅓ cup pickling salt
3 cups white vinegar
5 cups sugar
1½ teaspoons turmeric
1½ teaspoons celery seed
2 tablespoons mustard seed
¼ teaspoon cayenne pepper
3 tablespoons pickling spices (divided and tied in two cloth bags)

Wash cucumbers and slice very thin. Peel and slice onions. Cut peppers into narrow strips. Combine the vegetables and peeled garlic cloves in a large crockery bowl. Sprinkle the salt over the layers as you work. Mix a tray of ice cubes through the pickles and scatter another trayful over the top. Let stand for 3 hours. Add more ice as needed. It's the ice-salt mixture that makes the pickles especially crisp.

Sterilize canning jars and lids according to directions on page 5.

Drain the vegetables and discard the salt water. It is best to divide the pickles into two batches and cook in two kettles, each with half the syrup mixture. Cooking in small batches keeps them crisp and green. Combine vinegar, sugar, and spices. Pour over cucumber-vegetable slices, making sure each batch gets a bag of pickling spices. Heat just to boiling. That is all the cooking required. Pour into sterilized jars, leaving ½-inch headroom, and seal with sterilized lids according to manufacturer's instructions. Process in a boiling-water bath for 10 minutes. Let cure for about a month. This gives the flavors a chance to mingle.

YIELD: About 8 pints.

Myron Pestana
Patterson, California
Stanislaus
County Fair

Bread-and-Butter Pickles II

8 large cucumbers
8 small onions
2 large green bell peppers, cored and seeded
1 garlic clove
½ cup pickling salt
2 quarts cold water
1 quart ice cubes
4 cups sugar
3 cups white vinegar
1 tablespoon mustard seed
1 teaspoon celery seed
1 teaspoon ground turmeric

Slice cucumbers, onions, and green peppers very thin. Place vegetables and garlic clove in a crock or enamel pan and sprinkle with salt. Add the cold water and ice cubes and let stand 2 hours. Discard garlic and drain.

Sterilize canning jars and lids according to directions on page 5.

Combine sugar, vinegar, mustard seed, celery seed, and turmeric in a large kettle and bring to a boil. Add sliced vegetables and stir well. Return to a boil, quickly remove from heat, and pack into sterilized jars. Cover with syrup, leaving ½-inch headroom, and seal with sterilized lids according to manufacturer's instructions. Process in a boiling-water bath for 10 minutes.

YIELD: 6 pints.

Mrs. Perry Coy
Clovis, California
Fresno Fair

Crunchy Refrigerator Pickles

These pickles are stored in the refrigerator. They are not vacuum sealed or processed in a boiling-water bath, so you can keep them in wide-mouthed apothecary jars that come straight to the table. This recipe was handed down to Mrs. Lambeth from her great-grandmother.

8 cups thickly sliced cucumbers
2 small onions, sliced
1 small bell pepper, sliced
2 teaspoons pickling salt
2 cups white vinegar
2 cups sugar
1 teaspoon celery seed
1 teaspoon mustard seed

Combine cucumbers, onions, bell pepper, and salt and mix well. Put into jars. Combine vinegar, sugar, celery seed, and mustard seed in a saucepan. Cook over medium heat, stirring frequently, until sugar has dissolved. Pour, while still hot, over vegetables in jars. Let cool and refrigerate. These pickles will keep in the refrigerator for several months.

YIELD: 4 or 5 pints.

Mrs. Vae Lambeth
Winston-Salem,
North Carolina
Dixie Classic Fair

Ripe Cucumber Pickles

"My grandmother called these Tongue Pickles," writes Jane Zimmerman, "and they make a neat addition to the larder." This is a useful recipe for the gardener with end-of-summer bounty, but it is also worth making for its own sake.

9 large ripe cucumbers
⅓ cup pickling salt
4 cups white vinegar
2 cups sugar, or 1 cup honey
1 cinnamon stick per jar

Peel cucumbers and cut them in half lengthwise. Scrape out seeds and pulp and cut cucumbers into pieces that will fit in canning jars. Sprinkle cucumbers with salt and cover with cold water. Let stand overnight. Drain and rinse with fresh cold water. Drain again.

Sterilize canning jars and lids according to directions on page 5.

In a saucepan, combine vinegar and sugar or honey. Bring to a boil and cook 5 minutes. Add the drained cucumbers and return to a boil. Reduce heat and simmer until cucumbers are tender and appear translucent. Pour into sterilized jars, leaving ½-inch headroom, and seal with sterilized lids according to manufacturer's instructions. Process in a boiling-water bath for 10 minutes.

YIELD: 3 to 4 pints.

Jane Zimmerman
Oakfield, Maine
Common Ground
Country Fair

Easy Dill Pickles

1 flat pickling cucumbers (50 to 60)
1 whole garlic bulb
1 bunch fresh dill, or 1/4 teaspoon dill seed
1 quart white cider vinegar
1 cup pickling salt
1 tablespoon pickling spices
3 quarts water
Fresh grape leaves (optional)

Wash the cucumbers and discard any that are bruised. Sterilize canning jars and lids according to directions on page 5.

In each sterile jar place 1 garlic clove and a sprig of fresh dill or 1/4 teaspoon dill seed. Combine vinegar, salt, pickling spices, and water in a saucepan and boil for 5 minutes. Tightly pack cucumbers into jars and pour vinegar mixture over cucumbers, leaving 1/2-inch headspace. Top off each jar with a clean, folded grape leaf (for greener, crisper pickles) and seal with sterilized lids according to manufacturer's instructions. Process in a boiling-water bath for 10 minutes.

Let rest in brine for 2 to 3 months.

YIELD: 4 to 6 quarts.

Lois Haines
Fresno, California
The Big Fresno Fair

Triple Crown Dill Pickles

"When I was a new R.N., one of my patients was an elderly lady named Mae," writes Annamary Peck. "One day she said to me, 'Honey, you are so nice I am going to give you my pickle recipe. I'm called the pickle lady of Patterson, you know.' Mae has since passed on and it was several years before I tried her recipe, but when I did, the pickles took first prize at the county fair, and Best of Show, and the Ball Canning Award. Therefore I call them my Triple Crown Dill Pickles."

1 small hot red pepper per jar
1 cluster fresh dill per jar
2 garlic cloves per jar
30 to 36 medium-size canning cucumbers
3 cups white vinegar
3 cups water
6 tablespoons sea salt
1 teaspoon dill seed
1 teaspoon mustard seed

Sterilize canning jars and lids according to directions on page 5.

Put 1 hot red pepper, 1 cluster fresh dill, and 2 garlic cloves on the bottom of each sterilized jar. Wash cucumbers and pack into sterilized jars. In a saucepan, combine vinegar, water, salt, dill seed, and mustard seed. Bring to a boil and pour over cucumbers, leaving ½-inch headroom. Seal with sterilized lids according to manufacturer's instructions. Process in a boiling-water bath for 10 minutes.

YIELD: About 4 quarts.

Annamary Peck
Modesto, California
Stanislaus
County Fair

Sweet Pickles

16 cups sliced cucumbers
3¾ cups white vinegar
6 cups sugar
3 tablespoons pickling salt
4 teaspoons celery seed
2½ teaspoons turmeric
3 teaspoons mustard seed

Pour boiling water over the sliced cucumbers and let stand 3 hours.

Sterilize canning jars and lids according to directions on page 5.

Drain cucumbers and pack into sterile jars. Combine vinegar, sugar, salt, and spices in a saucepan and boil for 5 minutes. Pour boiling syrup over cucumbers in jars, leaving ½-inch headspace. Seal with sterilized lids according to manufacturer's instructions. Process in a boiling-water bath for 10 minutes.

YIELD: 6 pints.

LaVon McIntyre
White House, Tennessee
Tennessee State Fair

Seven-Day Sweet Pickles

"I really don't know where my family got this recipe," writes Mrs. Mishler, "I just know we have been making these pickles for as long as I can remember. They are easy to make and very good." The judges at three county fairs agreed with her and awarded a first prize.

7 pounds medium-size cucumbers
1 quart white vinegar
8 cups sugar
2 tablespoons pickling spices
2 tablespoons pickling salt

Wash cucumbers and cover with boiling water. Let stand 24 hours, then drain. Repeat each day for 4 days, using fresh water each day. On the 5th day, cut cucumbers into ¼-inch rings.

Combine vinegar, sugar, spices, and salt in a saucepan and bring to a boil. Pour over sliced cucumbers and let stand 24 hours. On 6th day, drain off syrup, bring to a boil, and pour over cucumbers. Let stand 24 hours.

On the last day, sterilize canning jars and lids according to directions on page 5.

Bring syrup to a boil, add cucumbers, and return to a boil. Pack into hot, sterilized jars, leaving ½-inch headroom, and seal with sterilized lids according to manufacturer's instructions. Process in a boiling-water bath for 10 minutes.

YIELD: 5 quarts.

Mrs. Merle Mishler
Hollsopple, Pennsylvania
Somerset County Fair
Cambria County Fair
Berlin Fair

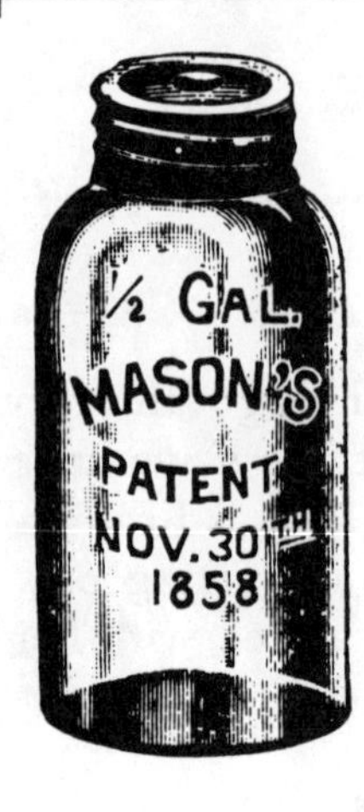

Mixed Pickled Vegetables

1 quart small cucumbers
3 to 4 carrots
3 celery stalks
2 red bell peppers
1 small cauliflower
2 cups peeled small white onions
1 cup pickling salt
4 quarts cold water
6½ cups white vinegar
2 cups sugar
¼ cup mustard seed
2 tablespoons celery seed
1 hot red pepper

Sterilize canning jars and lids according to directions on page 5.

Cut cucumbers into 1-inch slices. Peel carrots and cut them into 1½-inch slices. Cut celery into 1½-inch slices. Cut peppers into wide strips and break cauliflower into flowerets. Combine all the vegetables in a bowl or pot. Dissolve salt in the cold water. Pour over prepared vegetables. Let stand 12 to 18 hours in a cool place.

Combine vinegar, sugar, and spices in a large pot. Bring to a boil and boil for 3 minutes. Drain vegetables and add them to the boiling syrup. Simmer until all the vegetables are heated through. Pack, boiling hot, into sterilized hot jars, leaving ¼-inch headroom, and seal with sterilized lids according to manufacturer's instructions. Process in a boiling-water bath for 15 minutes.

YIELD: About 6 pints.

Barbara Carpenter
Milwaukee,
Wisconsin
Wisconsin
State Fair

Pickled Okra

3 pounds small, tender okra pods
1 small hot red pepper per jar
1 garlic clove per jar
1 pint white vinegar
1 quart water
¼ teaspoon pickling salt

Sterilize canning jars and lids according to directions on page 5.

Pack okra pods into hot, sterilized jars just tight enough to have them stand upright. Put 1 hot pepper and 1 garlic clove in each jar. Combine vinegar, water, and salt in a saucepan and bring to a boil. Pour boiling vinegar solution over okra, leaving ½-inch headroom. Seal with sterilized lids according to manufacturer's instructions. Process in a boiling-water bath at simmering temperature (180 to 200°F) for 10 minutes.

YIELD: 4 to 5 pints.

Mrs. W.O. McDaniel
Jonesboro, Arkansas
Craighead District Fair

Pickled Onions

Betty Welch has won more than fifty ribbons at the Arizona State Fair.

4 quarts small white onions
1½ cups pickling salt
1 gallon water
1 gallon white vinegar
1 cup sugar
1 small hot pepper per jar

Cover the onions with water. To each quart of water add 1 tablespoon salt. Soak for 2 hours. Drain and peel onions. Dissolve 1½ cups pickling salt in 1 gallon water and soak onions in this brine for 48 hours in a cool place.

Sterilize canning jars and lids according to directions on page 5. Drain onions.

Bring vinegar and sugar to a boil in a large pot. Add onions and boil for 3 minutes. Pack onions into sterilized jars, add 1 hot pepper to each jar, and cover with hot vinegar, leaving ½-inch headroom. Seal with sterilized lids according to manufacturer's instructions. Process in a boiling-water bath for 10 minutes.

YIELD: About 7 pints.

Betty Z. Welch
Phoenix, Arizona
Arizona State Fair

Pickled Peaches

These peaches taste best if they are chilled before serving.

12 to 16 medium-size peaches
(Clingstones are best but others will do)
Whole cloves
2 cups cider vinegar
2 cups sugar
6 cinnamon sticks

Sterilize canning jars and lids according to directions on page 5.

Dip each peach in boiling water to loosen skin, and remove the skins. Stick each peach with 4 to 5 cloves. Combine vinegar, sugar, and cinnamon in a pot large enough to hold the peaches and bring to a boil over medium heat. Drop peaches into boiling syrup and boil gently, over medium heat, until peaches are tender, 8 to 10 minutes. Pack them into hot, sterilized jars and add hot syrup, leaving 1/4-inch headroom. Seal with sterilized lids according to manufacturer's instructions. Process in a boiling-water bath for 20 minutes.

YIELD: 2 quarts.

Linda Strong
Tyler, Texas
East Texas Fair

Yellow Squash Pickles

8 cups thinly sliced yellow squash
2 cups thinly sliced onions
1 tablespoon pickling salt
1 cup cider vinegar
½ cup diced green bell peppers
1¾ cups sugar
½ teaspoon celery seed
½ teaspoon mustard seed

Sterilize canning jars and lids according to directions on page 5.

Combine squash, onions, and salt in a large bowl. Mix well and let stand for 1 hour. Combine vinegar, green peppers, sugar, celery seed, and mustard seed in a large saucepan and bring to a boil. Add squash and onions and bring to a boil again.

Pack pickles into hot, sterile jars. Cover with boiling vinegar mixture, leaving ½-inch headspace. Seal with sterilized lids according to manufacturer's instructions. Process in a boiling-water bath for 10 minutes.

YIELD: About 4 pints.

Deanna Odom
Raymond, Mississippi
Mississippi State Fair

Green Tomato Dill Pickles

Mrs. Walter enters the Michigan State Fair every year, following the tradition started by her mother in 1949.

5 pounds firm green tomatoes
(green cherry tomatoes make a lovely pickle)
1 fresh dill head or 2 tablespoons dill seed per jar
1 garlic clove per jar
1 whole clove per jar
1 dried hot red pepper per jar
1 quart white vinegar
1 quart water
½ cup pickling salt

Sterilize canning jars and lids according to directions on page 5.

Wash green tomatoes. If not using cherry tomatoes, slice ¼ inch thick. Place one fresh dill head in the bottom of each jar, or 2 tablespoons dill seed. Add 1 peeled garlic clove, 1 whole clove, and 1 dried hot red pepper per jar. Pack tomatoes loosely into jars. Combine vinegar, water, and salt in a saucepan and bring to a boil. Pour boiling liquid over tomatoes, leaving ½-inch headspace, and seal with sterilized lids according to manufacturer's instructions. Process in a boiling-water bath for 20 minutes.

YIELD: About 3 quarts.

Mrs. Charles L. Walter
Union Lake, Michigan
Michigan State Fair

Watermelon Rind Pickles

Here's a family recipe for an old-time classic.

7 pounds thick watermelon rind
¼ cup pickling salt
1 quart cold water
1 teaspoon granulated alum (optional)
7 cups sugar
2 cups white vinegar
½ teaspoon oil of cinnamon
½ teaspoon oil of cloves

Trim pink flesh and outer green from melon rind so you have white pulp. Cut pulp into 1-inch cubes. Dissolve salt in cold water and soak melon rind cubes in this solution overnight. Make more brine as needed to keep rind covered.

In the morning, drain the melon rind cubes, rinse, and drain again. Place in a large kettle and cover with cold water. Add the alum, if using, and cook until rind is tender but still crisp. Drain. Put in a crockery bowl.

Combine sugar, vinegar, oil of cinnamon, and oil of cloves in a saucepan. Bring to a boil and pour over rind. Cover and let stand overnight.

In the morning, sterilize canning jars and lids according to directions for sterilizing on page 5.

Drain off syrup into a saucepan. Pack the rind into sterilized canning jars. Bring syrup to a boil and pour over rind in jars, leaving ½-inch headspace. Seal with sterilized lids according to manufacturer's instructions. Process in a boiling-water bath for 10 minutes.

YIELD: About 8 pints.

Mrs. Christine Dziengel
Kennedy, Minnesota
Kittson County Fair

Zucchini Bread-and-Butter Pickles

18 small zucchini
4 medium-size onions
4 cups white vinegar
4 cups sugar
4 teaspoons pickling salt
4 teaspoons celery seed
4 teaspoons turmeric
¼ teaspoon alum powder (optional)

Sterilize canning jars and lids according to directions on page 5.

Slice zucchini and onions into very thin rounds. Combine vinegar, sugar, salt, celery seed, turmeric, and alum (if using) in a large kettle. Boil for 5 minutes. Add sliced zucchini and onions and return to a rolling boil. Remove from heat and pack into sterilized jars. Cover with syrup, leaving ½-inch headroom. Seal with sterilized lids according to manufacturer's instructions. Process in a boiling-water bath for 10 minutes.

YIELD: About 8 pints.

Annamary Peck
Modesto, California
Stanislaus
County Fair

Carrot Cucumber Relish

"This recipe is my own invention," writes Betty Mahan. "I will try to write it down as I make a batch for this year's fair."

10 medium-size carrots
8 medium-size onions
12 medium-size cucumbers
2 green bell peppers
2 red bell peppers
1 tablespoon hot red pepper flakes
½ to 1 cup pickling salt
4 to 5 cups apple cider vinegar
4 to 5 cups sugar (measure same as vinegar)
3 teaspoons mustard seed
1½ teaspoons celery seed

Coarsely grind or chop the vegetables with a meat grinder, food processor, or by hand. Combine vegetables and hot pepper flakes. In a bowl or crock, spread a layer of vegetables and sprinkle with salt. Continue adding layers of the vegetable mixture, sprinkling each with salt. Let stand overnight, then drain well.

Sterilize canning jars and lids according to directions on page 5.

Put vinegar, sugar, mustard seed, and celery seed in a large pot and bring to a boil. Add the vegetables and simmer for 15 minutes. Pour into hot, sterilized jars, leaving ½-inch headroom, and seal with sterilized lids according to manufacturer's instructions. Process in a boiling-water bath for 10 minutes.

YIELD: 6 to 8 pints.

Betty Mahan
Rough and Ready, California
Nevada County Fair

Sweet Chow Chow

"I've entered this in the Tennessee State Fair going on fourteen years and I've won first place ten times," writes LaVon McIntyre. She adds that she got this recipe from a friend twenty years ago.

12 green tomatoes
1 large cabbage
7 medium-size onions
12 green bell peppers
6 red bell peppers
½ cup pickling salt
6 cups sugar
1 tablespoon celery seed
2 tablespoons mustard seed
1½ teaspoons turmeric
4 cups cider vinegar (5 percent acidity)

Grind tomatoes, cabbage, onions, and green and red bell peppers into a large pan—or process in a food processor in small batches. Add salt and let stand overnight. Rinse and drain.

Sterilize canning jars and lids according to directions on page 5.

Put the drained vegetables into a large kettle, add the remaining ingredients, and bring to a boil. Boil for 8 minutes, stirring constantly. Pour into sterilized jars, leaving ½-inch headroom, and seal with sterilized lids according to manufacturer's instructions. Process in a boiling-water bath for 10 minutes. Let stand at least 2 weeks before opening.

YIELD: 7 pints.

Note: For hot chow chow, add 10 hot peppers and 1 tablespoon cayenne pepper.

LaVon McIntyre
White House, Tennessee
Tennessee State Fair

Corn Relish I

"With economic times as they are," writes Malinda Lifer, "my garden goes a long way toward feeding our family all year." Her prizewinning recipe for corn relish is an old family favorite.

9 medium-size ears of corn, shucked
1 quart white vinegar
1 cup sugar
1 tablespoon pickling salt
1½ tablespoons dry mustard
1 teaspoon turmeric
1 small cabbage, coarsely ground or chopped
2 medium-size white onions, chopped
3 red bell peppers, seeded and chopped
2 green bell peppers, seeded and chopped

Sterilize canning jars and lids according to directions on page 5.

Cook corn in boiling water for 2 minutes. Remove the corn, dip into cold water, and cut the kernels away from the cob.

Combine vinegar, sugar, salt, mustard, and turmeric in a large pot and bring to a boil. Add the corn and other vegetables and simmer for 20 to 30 minutes (until vegetables are tender), stirring frequently. Pour into hot, sterilized jars, leaving ½-inch headroom, and seal with sterilized lids according to manufacturer's instructions. Process in a boiling-water bath for 15 minutes.

YIELD: About 8 pints.

Malinda Lifer
Lancaster, Ohio
Fairfield
County Fair

Corn Relish II

5 packages (10 ounces each) frozen corn kernels, or 7 cups fresh corn kernels
2 cups chopped onions
2 cups white corn syrup
2 cups white vinegar
1 cup sugar
1 cup water
2 tablespoons mustard seed
1 teaspoon pickling salt
1½ teaspoons celery seed
2 cups seeded and chopped green bell pepper
2 cups seeded and chopped red bell pepper

Sterilize canning jars and lids according to directions on page 5.

Combine corn kernels, onions, corn syrup, vinegar, sugar, water, mustard seed, salt, and celery seed in a large pot. Bring to a boil and boil for 10 minutes, stirring frequently. Add the chopped peppers and return to a boil.

Pour into hot, sterilized jars, leaving ½-inch headroom, and seal with sterilized lids according to manufacturer's instructions. Process in a boiling-water bath for 15 minutes.

YIELD: 6 pints.

Janina Seyfert
Glendale, Wisconsin
Wisconsin State Fair

Golden Relish

3 cups shredded carrots
1½ cups chopped onions
¾ cup finely chopped green bell pepper
¾ cup finely chopped red bell pepper
¾ cup finely chopped cabbage
¼ cup chopped celery
2 cups apple cider vinegar
1 cup light corn syrup
1 cup water
½ cup sugar
1 tablespoon pickling salt
½ teaspoon celery seed
1½ teaspoons mustard seed

Sterilize canning jars and lids according to directions on page 5.

In a large pot, combine carrots, onions, green and red peppers, cabbage, and celery. Cover with boiling water and let stand 5 minutes. Drain and return the vegetables to the pot. Add vinegar, corn syrup, water, sugar, salt, celery seed, and mustard seed. Over medium-high heat, bring to a boil, stirring occasionally. Reduce heat to low, cover, and simmer for 20 minutes. Remove cover, raise heat to medium-high, and cook, stirring, until liquid is reduced and barely covers vegetables. Pour into hot, sterilized jars, leaving ½-inch headroom, and seal with sterilized lids according to manufacturer's instructions. Process in a boiling-water bath for 10 minutes.

YIELD: 4 to 5 pints.

Opal M. Reed
Tyler, Texas
Smith County Fair

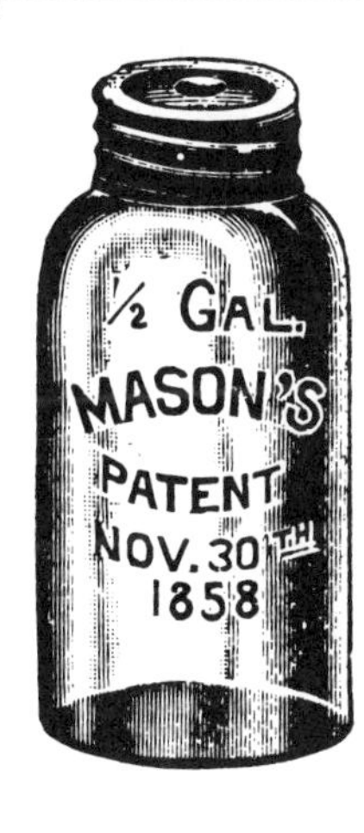

India Relish

Mrs. Mishler got this recipe from an aunt who found it in an old church cookbook "years back." She makes it in quantity every year because her family loves it on hot dogs and hamburgers, and it always wins prizes at the county fair.

2 gallons green tomatoes
12 bell peppers (red or green)
12 large onions
1 quart white vinegar
2 sticks cinnamon
2 tablespoons whole allspice
2 tablespoons whole cloves
2 tablespoons pickling salt
2 tablespoons mustard seed
1 teaspoon celery seed
4 cups sugar

Sterilize canning jars and lids according to directions on page 5.

Chop all the vegetables into very small pieces, or put them through a food grinder or processor. Put them in a large pot and bring to a slow boil (over medium heat), stirring frequently. Boil for 15 minutes, stirring occasionally. Remove from heat and drain in a colander.

In a saucepan, combine vinegar, cinnamon, allspice, and cloves. Bring to a rapid boil (over high heat) and boil for 5 minutes. Strain out all the spices and combine vinegar with the vegetables in saucepan. Add salt, mustard seed, celery seed, and sugar. Bring to a boil and boil for 1 minute. Pour into hot, sterilized jars, leaving ½-inch headroom, and seal with sterilized lids according to manufacturer's instructions. Process in a boiling-water bath for 10 minutes.

YIELD: 8 pints.

Mrs. Merle Mishler
Hollsopple, Pennsylvania
Somerset County Fair

Sweet Hot Pear Relish

This original relish has won many blue ribbons.

25 large hard pears
12 large bell peppers
12 large onions
6 carrots
12 hot red peppers
3 cups sugar
2 cups white vinegar
2 tablespoons pickling salt
2 tablespoons mustard seed
2 tablespoons celery seed

Peel and core the pears. Core and slice the bell peppers. Peel onions and cut into large chunks. Scrape and wash the carrots. Grind all the vegetables together in a food grinder or food processor. Mix together with remaining ingredients in a large saucepan. Bring to a boil and simmer slowly, stirring frequently, for 1½ hours.

Sterilize canning jars and lids according to directions on page 5.

Fill jars with boiling relish, leaving ½-inch headspace. Seal with sterilized lids according to manufacturer's instructions. Process in a boiling-water bath for 10 minutes.

YIELD: 9 to 10 pints.

Lynda Bentley
Nacogdoches, Texas
Nacogdoches
County Fair

Bell Pepper Relish

6 green bell peppers
6 red bell peppers
6 large yellow onions
1 cup sugar
1 cup white vinegar
1½ teaspoons dill seed
1½ teaspoons pickling salt

Sterilize canning jars and lids according to directions on page 5.

Finely grind peppers and onions. Drain well. In a saucepan, mix peppers and onions and cover with boiling water. Let stand 5 minutes. Drain. Add sugar, vinegar, dill seed, salt, and ½ cup water. Bring to a boil and boil gently, stirring frequently, for 5 minutes. Pour into sterilized jars, leaving ½-inch headroom, and seal with sterilized lids according to manufacturer's instructions. Process in a boiling-water bath for 5 minutes.

YIELD: 10 half pints.

Diana Yarbrough
Jacksonville, Florida
Greater Jacksonville Agricultural Fair

Christmas Pepper Relish

"This recipe was sent to me by my cousin in Puerto Rico," writes Opal Reed. It won first place at the Smith County Fair.

5 red bell peppers
4 green bell peppers
¾ cup white vinegar
2 tablespoons whole pickling spices (tied in cheesecloth)
½ teaspoon Tabasco sauce
½ teaspoon butter
1 package (1¾ ounces) powdered fruit pectin
3 cups sugar

Sterilize canning jars and lids according to directions on page 5.

Grind red and green peppers in a food grinder or processor and set aside in a colander to drain. In a large saucepan, combine peppers, vinegar, spices, Tabasco, and butter. Stir pectin into this mixture and bring to a full rolling boil over high heat, stirring constantly. Immediately add sugar and continue boiling, stirring continuously, for 1 minute. Remove from heat, pour into hot, sterilized jars, leaving ½-inch headroom, and seal with sterilized lids according to manufacturer's instructions. Process in a boiling-water bath for 10 minutes.

YIELD: 5 to 6 half pints.

Opal M. Reed
Tyler, Texas
Smith County Fair

Red Pepper Relish

2 dozen red bell peppers
7 medium-size onions
2 tablespoons mustard seed
2 tablespoons pickling salt
3 cups white vinegar
3 cups sugar

Sterilize canning jars and lids according to directions on page 5.

Grind the peppers and onions, saving the juice, or cut into chunks and process in a food processor. Combine all the ingredients in a large pot. Bring to a boil and cook over medium heat, stirring frequently, for 30 minutes. Pack into hot, sterilized jars, leaving ½-inch headroom, and seal with sterilized lids according to manufacturer's instructions. Process in a boiling-water bath for 10 minutes.

YIELD: About 10 half pints.

Deanna Odom
Raymond, Mississippi
Mississippi State Fair

Pittsfield Sauce

The recipe for this sweet relish came from Claire Gregory's great aunt, who lived in Massachusetts and New Hampshire. It is delicious with all kinds of food besides hot dogs and hamburgers, and Mrs. Gregory's family will not eat baked beans without some Pittsfield Sauce to go with them.

1 large cabbage, cut into chunks
1 large bunch celery, cut into chunks
3 red bell peppers, cut into chunks
4 cups diced onions
6 cups diced green tomatoes
6 cups diced red ripe tomatoes
½ cup pickling salt
1 teaspoon cinnamon
1 teaspoon cloves
½ cup mustard seed
6 cups sugar
6 cups cider vinegar

Grind cabbage, celery, sweet peppers, onions, green tomatoes, and red tomatoes in a food grinder or processor. Combine with salt in a large enamel or stainless steel bowl. Mix and let stand for 24 hours.

Drain thoroughly and combine in a large saucepan with cinnamon, cloves, mustard seed, sugar, and vinegar. Bring to a boil, then simmer for 1½ hours, stirring frequently with a large wooden spoon.

Sterilize canning jars and lids according to directions on page 5.

Pour hot sauce into hot, sterilized jars, leaving ½-inch headroom, and seal with sterilized lids according to manufacturer's instructions. Process in a boiling-water bath for 10 minutes.

YIELD: 9 to 10 half pints.

Mrs. Claire L. Gregory
Vallejo, California
Solano County Fair and Napa County Fair

Grandma Hurley's Green Tomato Relish

"This relish recipe was passed down to me from Grandma Hurley of Henry, South Dakota," Irene Kverne writes. "She was not my grandma but the grandmother of the kids living on a neighboring farm. I have used the recipe for forty-five canning seasons. All who taste it find it to be a delicious relish, ideal for meats and great for mixing with salad dressing for sandwich spread and dips. It has won a blue ribbon in the Central States Fair every year it was entered."

1 gallon green tomatoes
½ gallon onions
½ cup pickling salt
2 quarts cold water
1 quart white vinegar
2 pounds sugar
2 teaspoons black pepper
2 teaspoons whole mustard seed
2 teaspoons ground cloves
1 teaspoon celery seed
2 cinnamon sticks

Core and slice the tomatoes. Peel and slice the onions. Dissolve salt in cold water and pour over the vegetables. Let stand overnight. In the morning, drain and run through a food grinder or processor.

Sterilize canning jars and lids according to directions on page 5.

In a large pot, combine tomatoes, onions, vinegar, sugar, and spices. Bring to a boil and boil for 15 minutes. Pour into hot, sterilized jars, leaving ½-inch headroom, and seal with sterilized lids according to manufacturer's instructions. Process in a boiling-water bath for 10 minutes.

YIELD: About 7 pints.

Irene Kverne
Rapid City, South Dakota
Central States Fair

Zucchini Relish I

"I am happy to share this recipe," writes Beverly Conway. "It was given to me by my Aunt Betty in Ohio. It is wonderful on hamburger and straight from the spoon to the mouth."

10 cups unpeeled, finely chopped zucchini
1 large onion, chopped fine
5 tablespoons pickling salt
1 red bell pepper, chopped fine
1 green bell pepper, chopped fine
4 celery stalks, chopped fine
4 cups sugar
2¼ cups white vinegar
1 teaspoon dry mustard
1 teaspoon celery seed
1 teaspoon turmeric

Mix together chopped zucchini, chopped onion, and salt. Cover and let stand overnight.

Sterilize canning jars and lids according to directions on page 5.

Drain the vegetables and combine in a large pot with remaining ingredients. Bring to a boil, lower heat, and simmer for 3 minutes. Pack into sterilized jars, leaving ½-inch headroom, and seal with sterilized lids according to manufacturer's instructions. Process in a boiling-water bath for 10 minutes.

YIELD: 4 pints.

Beverly Conway
Hallandale, Florida
Broward County Fair

Zucchini Relish II

"My family likes this better than pickle relish, and it is a favorite recipe to make up each year as the zucchini become ripe," writes Connie Betz.

10 cups chopped zucchini*
3 to 4 medium-size onions, chopped
4 tablespoons pickling salt
2½ cups white vinegar
6 cups sugar
1 tablespoon turmeric
2 tablespoons cornstarch
2 tablespoons celery seed
3 to 4 green bell peppers, chopped

***If zucchini is very large, peel and remove seeds.**

Combine zucchini, onions, and salt in a pan. Mix well and let sit overnight. The next day, drain and rinse well. Drain again.

Sterilize canning jars and lids according to directions on page 5.

In a large pot, combine zucchini and onions with remaining ingredients. Bring to a boil, reduce heat, and simmer for 30 minutes, stirring frequently to prevent sticking. Pour into hot, sterilized jars, leaving ½-inch headroom, and seal with sterilized lids according to manufacturer's instructions. Process in a boiling-water bath for 10 minutes.

YIELD: 6 pints.

Connie L. Betz
Compton, Illinois
The Tri-County Fair

Zucchini Relish III

I received more recipes for Zucchini Relish than for any other relish or pickle. It seems that almost every family with a garden has its own recipe. This relish is a little spicier than most.

10 cups ground or finely chopped zucchini
4 cups ground or finely chopped onion
2 green bell peppers, ground or finely chopped
1 red bell pepper, ground or finely chopped
5 tablespoons pickling salt
5 cups sugar
3 cups white vinegar
1 tablespoon turmeric
¼ teaspoon chili powder
⅛ teaspoon cayenne pepper
1 tablespoon cornstarch
1 tablespoon nutmeg
1 teaspoon black pepper
1 tablespoon dry mustard
1 tablespoon celery seed

Combine ground vegetables and sprinkle with salt. Mix well and let sit overnight. Drain in a colander lined with cheesecloth. Rinse well and let drain again.

Sterilize canning jars and lids according to directions on page 5.

In a large pot, combine vegetables with remaining ingredients. Bring to a boil, reduce heat, and simmer for 30 minutes, stirring frequently. Pour into sterilized jars, leaving ½-inch headroom, and seal with sterilized lids according to manufacturer's instructions. Process in a boiling-water bath for 10 minutes.

YIELD: About 6 pints.

Debra Horinek
Kalispell, Montana
Northwest Montana Fair

PRESERVES

Including Jams, Conserves, Jellies, Butters, and Chutneys

Apple Butter

3½ to 4 pounds apples
(about 10 medium-size apples)
Apple cider or apple juice
2 cups sugar
⅛ teaspoon salt
⅛ teaspoon nutmeg
¼ teaspoon cinnamon
¼ teaspoon ground cloves

Wash the apples, peel and slice them. Using an equal measure of fruit and apple cider or apple juice, combine apples and cider or juice in a large kettle. Simmer over medium heat until fruit is soft, stirring frequently (20 to 30 minutes). Press through a food mill or a sieve to remove all fibrous material and give a smooth consistency.

Measure 4 cups of apple pulp. Combine with sugar, salt, and spices in a large heavy pot and bring to a boil. Continue to boil rapidly, stirring constantly to prevent sticking. As the butter cooks down and thickens, reduce the heat to prevent spattering. Continue cooking until desired thickness is reached. This takes from 1 to 1½ hours.

Sterilize canning jars and lids according to directions on page 5.

Pour apple butter into hot, sterilized jars, leaving ½-inch headroom, and seal with sterilized lids according to manufacturer's instructions. Process in a boiling-water bath for 10 minutes.

YIELD: 4 half pints.

Polly Townsend
Forney, Texas
State Fair of Texas

Crock Pot Apple Butter

"My grandmother gave me this apple butter recipe," writes Alice Thiele. "But I improved on her methods by cooking it in the crock pot. I received Best of Show on my apple butter two years in a row." Make this delicious butter when good apples are abundant.

Apples
Sugar
Cinnamon

Core and slice apples, but do *not* peel. Cook apples, covered, in a large pot, over very low heat, until they are tender. Do not add liquid; they will make their own. Strain apples through a sieve or press through a food mill, to remove peeling. Measure the apple sauce, then measure sugar to equal 1 cup more than half the amount of applesauce. For example: For 8 cups applesauce, use 5 cups sugar. For 10 cups applesauce, use 6 cups sugar. Add cinnamon to taste, about 1 tablespoon. Combine applesauce, sugar, and cinnamon in crock pot and mix well. Cook *uncovered* on high for 5 hours (high on a crock pot is 300°F).

Sterilize canning jars and lids according to directions on page 5.

Ladle apple butter into hot, sterilized jars, leaving ½-inch headroom, and seal with sterilized lids according to manufacturer's instructions. Process in a boiling-water bath for 10 minutes. Or put in airtight containers and freeze.

YIELD: 8 cups of applesauce will yield about 5 pints.

Alice P. Thiele
Brandon, South Dakota
Sioux Empire Fair and Minnehaha County Fair

Blender Spicy Apple Butter

Charlotte Davis has been exhibiting in fairs since her high school days in 1922. She won first sweepstakes in home economics at the Siskiyou Golden Fair twenty times, twelve of which have been in the last twelve years. She says that for best results in making her apple butter, use tart apples.

3 pounds firm, ripe apples
2 cups water
7½ cups sugar
1 teaspoon ground allspice
1½ teaspoons cinnamon
¼ cup lemon juice
1 pouch (3 ounces) liquid fruit pectin

Sterilize canning jars and lids according to directions on page 5.

Peel, core, and slice apples into eighths. Place one quarter of the apple slices and ½ cup water in an electric blender. Blend at high speed for about 15 seconds. Repeat with remaining apples and water. You should have about 5 cups of apple pulp.

Place apple pulp in a large saucepan. Add sugar, spices, and lemon juice. Bring to a full, rolling boil and boil for 1 minute, stirring constantly. Remove from heat and stir in pectin at once. Skim off any foam. Pour into canning jars, leaving ½-inch headspace, and seal with canning lids according to manufacturer's instructions. Process in a boiling-water bath for 10 minutes.

YIELD: About 2½ pints.

Mrs. Charlotte Davis
Montague, California
Siskiyou Golden Fair

Apple Marmalade

1 medium-size orange
6 medium-size apples, peeled, cored, and coarsely chopped (about 6 cups)
2 cups water
3 tablespoons lemon juice
5 cups sugar

Sterilize canning jars and lids according to directions on page 5.

Quarter the unpeeled orange and remove the seeds. Cut into thin slices. In an 8- to 10-quart kettle or dutch oven, combine orange slices, apples, water, and lemon juice. Bring mixture to a boil. Reduce heat and simmer about 10 minutes, or until apples are tender. Add sugar and stir well. Bring to a full rolling boil, stirring until thickened and clear (220°F on a candy thermometer, or until syrup sheets from the spoon as described in the jelly test, page 6). Remove from heat. Skim off foam with a metal spoon. Pour at once into sterilized jars, leaving ½-inch headroom, and seal with sterilized lids according to manufacturer's instructions. Process in a boiling-water bath for 10 minutes.

YIELD: 6 half pints.

Jennette Smith
Turlock, California
Stanislaus
County Fair

Apple Honey Jelly

6 cups peeled, cored, and sliced apples
4 cups honey

Sterilize canning jars and lids according to directions on page 5.

Combine apples and honey in a large saucepan and cook over high heat, stirring frequently, until lots of small bubbles appear. Continue cooking until syrup sheets from the spoon as described in the jelly test, page 6. Remove from heat and skim off foam with a metal spoon. Pour at once into sterilized jars, leaving ½-inch headroom, and seal with sterilized lids according to manufacturer's instructions.

YIELD: 5 or 6 half pints.

Jane Zimmerman
Oakfield, Maine
Common Ground
County Fair

Apple Kiwi Jelly

3 kiwis
1 can (6 ounces) frozen apple juice concentrate (thawed)
1 package (1¾ ounces) powdered fruit pectin
2 cups sugar

Sterilize canning jars and lids according to directions on page 5.

Peel kiwis and place them in a food processor or blender together with the apple juice and water. Blend to a purée. In a pot, combine kiwi mixture with pectin. Bring to a boil, stirring frequently to keep from sticking. Add sugar and boil 3 to 5 minutes. Remove from heat. Pour at once into sterilized jars, leaving ½-inch headroom, and seal with sterilized lids according to manufacturer's instructions.

YIELD: About 4 half pints.

Opal M. Reed
Tyler, Texas
Smith County Fair

Apricot Butter

5 pounds apricots
6 cups sugar
Juice and grated rind of 1 orange
¼ teaspoon ground cloves
½ teaspoon cinnamon

Sterilize canning jars and lids according to directions on page 5.

Drop apricots into boiling water for 1 minute to loosen the skins. Peel and pit apricots and cut into small pieces. Add sugar, orange rind, juice, cloves, and cinnamon. Simmer over low heat, stirring frequently, until mixture is thick enough to spread, 1 to 1½ hours. Pour into sterilized jars, leaving ½-inch headroom, and seal with sterilized lids according to manufacturer's instructions. Process in a boiling-water bath for 10 minutes.

YIELD: About 10 half pints.

Vicki Lynch
Granada Hills,
California
Los Angeles
County Fair

Apricot Preserves

5 cups firm ripe apricots, halved and peeled (about 2 pounds)
4 cups sugar
¼ cup lemon juice

Thoroughly mix fruit with sugar and lemon juice. Cover and let stand 4 to 5 hours in a cool place.

Sterilize canning jars and lids according to directions on page 5.

Heat apricot mixture slowly to boiling, stirring occasionally until sugar dissolves. Cook at a low boil until fruit is clear, about 30 minutes. As mixture thickens, stir frequently to prevent sticking. Pour into hot, sterilized jars, leaving ½-inch headroom, and seal with sterilized lids according to manufacturer's instructions. Process in a boiling-water bath for 15 minutes.

YIELD: About 4½ pints.

Polly Townsend
Forney, Texas
State Fair of Texas

Basil Jelly

3 cups apple juice
1½ cups firmly packed crushed fresh basil leaves
2 tablespoons cider vinegar
1 or 2 drops green food coloring (optional)
3½ cups sugar
1 pouch (3 ounces) liquid fruit pectin

Sterilize canning jars and lids according to directions on page 5.

Bring 1 cup apple juice to a rolling boil and pour over crushed basil leaves. Let stand for 20 minutes. Strain into a large saucepan. Add remaining apple juice, vinegar, and food coloring, if desired. Mix in sugar and bring to a boil. Stir in pectin, return to a full rolling boil, and boil for 1 minute. Remove from heat and skim off foam with a metal spoon. Pour into sterilized jars, leaving ½-inch headroom, and seal with sterilized lids according to manufacturer's instructions.

YIELD: 3 to 4 half pints.

Sheila Allison
Clovis, California
Fresno Fair

Beet Jelly

This unusual family recipe produces a jelly of an astonishing color and lovely taste.

3 cups beet juice (the water in which beets have been cooked)
1 package (1¾ ounces) powdered fruit pectin
3½ cups sugar
1 package raspberry Kool-Aid

Sterilize canning jars and lids according to directions on page 5.

Place beet juice and pectin in a large saucepan and bring to a boil. Boil for 1 minute. Add sugar and Kool-Aid. Boil for 3 minutes. Remove from heat and skim if necessary. Pour into sterilized jars, leaving ½-inch headroom, and seal with sterilized lids according to manufacturer's instructions.

YIELD: About 6 half pints.

Marjorie Sperling
Walbach, Nebraska
Howard
County Fair

Blackberry Jam

9 cups crushed blackberries
6 cups sugar

Sterilize canning jars and lids according to directions on page 5.

Combine berries and sugar in a large saucepan. Bring slowly to a boil, stirring occasionally until sugar dissolves. Cook rapidly to, or almost to, jellying point, depending on whether a firm or soft jam is desired. As mixture thickens, stir frequently to prevent sticking. Pour boiling hot into sterilized jars, leaving ½-inch headroom, and seal with sterilized jars according to manufacturer's instructions. Process in a boiling-water bath for 10 minutes.

YIELD: 3 to 4 pints.

Note: If seedless jam is preferred, crushed berries should be cooked until soft and pressed through a sieve or food mill; then add sugar and proceed as above.

Dorothy Watts
Rantoul, Illinois
Greater Champaign
County Fair

Blackberry Jelly

2½ quarts fully ripe blackberries
¼ cup lemon juice
7½ cups sugar
2 pouches (6 ounces) liquid fruit pectin

Sterilize canning jars and lids according to directions on page 5.

Crush the berries and strain them through a jelly bag to get 4 cups juice. If you are slightly short of juice, add a little bit of water to the pulp in the jelly bag. Combine blackberry juice with lemon juice and sugar in a large saucepan. Mix well. Bring to a boil over high heat, stirring constantly. Immediately stir in pectin and return to a full rolling boil, stirring constantly. Remove from heat and skim off foam with a metal spoon. Pour into sterilized jars, leaving ½-inch headroom, and seal with sterilized jars according to manufacturer's instructions.

YIELD: 8 half pints.

Jeanne Kinney
Marston Mills,
Massachusetts
Barnstable
County Fair

Blackberry Honey Jelly

This recipe calls for whole berries instead of juice, and honey instead of sugar.

4 cups ripe blackberries
4 cups honey

Sterilize canning jars and lids according to directions on page 5.

Sort and wash berries. Remove any stems, caps, or bruised berries. Combine berries and honey in a large saucepan and cook until lots of small bubbles appear. Continue cooking until jelly mixture sheets from a spoon as described in jelly test, page 6. Pour hot jelly into sterilized jars, leaving ½-inch headroom, and seal with sterilized lids according to manufacturer's instructions.

YIELD: 5 or 6 half pints.

Jane Zimmerman
Oakfield, Maine
Common Ground
County Fair

Blueberry Jam

3 quarts blueberries
3 cups sugar

Sterilize canning jars and lids according to directions on page 5.

Use only fresh, ripe, unbruised berries. Wash and drain thoroughly. Crush the blueberries and measure the pulp and liquid. You should have about 3 pints. Measure 1 cup of sugar for every pint of pulp. Combine crushed blueberries and sugar in a large kettle and bring slowly to a boil (over medium heat), stirring occasionally until sugar dissolves. When all sugar has dissolved, raise heat to high and cook rapidly until thick. Stir frequently to prevent sticking or burning. Remove from heat and skim off foam with a metal spoon. Pour into hot, sterilized jars, leaving ½-inch headroom, and seal with sterilized lids according to manufacturer's instructions. Process in a boiling-water bath for 10 minutes.

YIELD: 6 half pints.

Jane Autumn Lewis
Farmington Hills,
Michigan
Michigan State Fair

Blueberry Freezer Jam

Because this jam is not cooked, it retains a fresh, clear, fruity taste.

¼ cup powdered fruit pectin
2 tablespoons sugar
1 cup blueberries, mashed
¾ cup sugar
2 tablespoons corn syrup
2 tablespoons lemon juice

Combine pectin and 2 tablespoons sugar. Stir into blueberries in a mixer bowl. Add remaining ingredients. Beat at low speed for 7 minutes. Pour into jelly jars and cover. Let stand overnight at room temperature. Store in freezer.

Irene Haas
Arenac, Michigan
Michigan 4-H

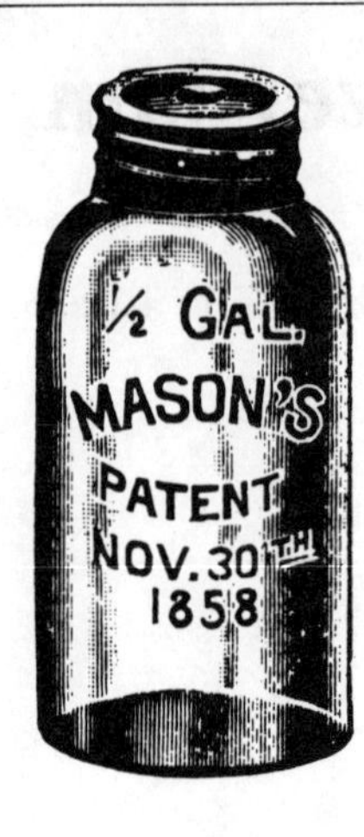

Cantaloupe Pear Honey

3 pounds ripe pears
½ ripe cantaloupe
Juice from 1 lemon
4 cups sugar

Sterilize canning jars and lids according to directions on page 5.

Wash, peel, and core the pears. Chop them into very small pieces by hand, or in a blender or food processor. You should have about 9 cups chopped pears. Peel and seed the cantaloupe. Cut into small pieces and purée in blender or food processor. Combine pears, cantaloupe, and lemon juice in a large saucepan. Add the sugar and cook over low heat, stirring often, for 15 to 20 minutes.

Pour into sterilized jars, leaving ½-inch headroom, and seal with sterilized lids according to manufacturer's instructions. Process in a boiling-water bath for 10 minutes.

YIELD: About 5 half pints.

Note: The mixture can be strained to eliminate fruit pieces if desired. Strain first, then pour into hot, sterilized jars.

Opal Reed
Tyler, Texas
Smith County Fair

Carrot Marmalade

1 pound carrots
2 medium-size oranges
Juice of 4 medium-size lemons
7 cups sugar
1 pouch (3 ounces) liquid fruit pectin

Sterilize canning jars and lids according to directions on page 5.

Wash, peel, and shred carrots (this is best done in a food processor). Place shredded carrots in a large pot. Seed the oranges, chop them, and add them to the pot. Add lemon juice and sugar. Bring to a rapid boil that cannot be stirred down and boil for 5 minutes, stirring constantly. Remove from heat and stir in pectin. Skim and stir for 5 minutes to keep carrots from floating. Pour into sterilized jars, leaving ½-inch headroom, and seal with sterilized lids according to manufacturer's instructions. Process in a boiling-water bath for 10 minutes.

YIELD: About 5 half pints.

Sonia Anderson
Alameda, California
California
State Fair

Cherry Preserves

2 pounds pitted tart cherries
4 cups sugar

Drain juice from cherries. Add sugar to juice (if there is not enough juice to dissolve the sugar, add a little water) and cook slowly, until sugar dissolves. Stir the mixture occasionally to keep it from sticking. Cool. Add the cherries and cook rapidly until they become glossy, about 15 minutes. Cover and let stand 12 to 18 hours in a cool place.

Sterilize canning jars and lids according to directions on page 5.

Bring cherries to a hard boil and boil for 1 minute. Pour boiling hot into sterilized jars, leaving ½-inch headroom, and seal with sterilized lids according to manufacturer's instructions. Process in a boiling-water bath for 10 minutes.

YIELD: About 4 half pints.

Dorothy Watts
Rantoul, Illinois
Greater Champaign County Fair

Chokecherry Jelly

A chokecherry is a native American wild cherry that is considered too tart to eat raw, but makes a superb jelly. This is a family recipe.

3 pounds (approximately) chokecherries
¼ cup water
1 package (1¾ ounces) powdered fruit pectin
4½ cups sugar

Sterilize canning jars and lids according to directions on page 5.

Wash the cherries and remove the stems. Place them in a large pot and crush them. Do not remove the pits. Add ¼ cup water and bring to a boil. Reduce heat and simmer for 10 to 15 minutes. Strain cherries and all the liquid through a jelly bag.

Measure 3½ cups juice and combine with pectin in a saucepan. Bring to a hard boil over high heat, stirring occasionally. Immediately add sugar and return to a full, rolling boil. Boil hard for 1 minute, stirring constantly. Remove from heat and skim off foam with a metal spoon. Pour at once into sterilized jars, leaving ½-inch headroom, and seal with sterilized lids according to manufacturer's instructions.

YIELD: About 5 half pints.

Marjorie Sperling
Walbach, Nebraska
Howard
County Fair

Corncob Jelly

This family recipe reflects the thrifty practices of a bygone era when even the cobs that remained after the corn kernels were consumed were put to use. It makes a lovely clear jelly with a mild honey-like flavor.

12 to 14 large red corncobs (you may substitute yellow or white corncobs)
1 package (1¾ ounces) powdered fruit pectin
3 cups sugar

Sterilize canning jars and lids according to directions on page 5.

Wash the cobs well in cold water and break them into chunks. Put them in a large saucepan and cover completely with about 3 pints water. Boil for 45 minutes, or until liquid has reduced by almost half. Strain off 3 cups of liquid and place in a smaller saucepan. Add pectin and bring to a boil. Add sugar and boil for 1 minute. Skim the mixture. Pour into hot, sterilized jars, leaving ½-inch headroom, and seal with sterilized lids according to manufacturer's instructions.

YIELD: About 4 half pints.

Marjorie Sperling
Walbach, Nebraska
Howard
County Fair

Crab Apple Jelly

5 pounds crab apples
5 cups water
1 package (1¾ ounces) powdered fruit pectin
9 cups sugar

Wash and remove stems and blossom ends from crab apples. Cut apples into small pieces, combine with water, cover, and boil about 15 minutes. Stir apples occasionally to keep them from burning. Pour apples through a jelly bag and let drain until you have 7 cups juice. Do not squeeze the jelly bag. Squeezing the bag will make cloudy jelly.

Sterilize canning jars and lids according to directions on page 5.

Combine apple juice and pectin in a large pot. Bring to a boil over high heat, stirring constantly. Stir in sugar and return to a full rolling boil. Boil for 1 minute, stirring continuously. Remove from heat and skim off foam with a metal spoon. Pour into sterilized jars, leaving ½-inch headroom, and seal with sterilized lids according to manufacturer's instructions.

YIELD: About 10 half pints.

Mrs. Ruth Baird
Lancaster,
Massachusetts
Sterling Fair
Bolton Fair

Cranberry Conserve

1 unpeeled orange, finely chopped
2 cups water
1 quart stemmed cranberries
½ cup seedless raisins
3 cups sugar
½ cups chopped walnuts (or other nuts)

Sterilize canning jars and lids according to directions on page 5.

Combine chopped orange and water. Cook rapidly until peel is tender, about 20 minutes. Add cranberries, raisins, and sugar. Bring slowly to a boil, stirring occasionally until sugar dissolves. Cook at a rapid boil almost to jelly stage, about 8 minutes. As mixture thickens, stir frequently to prevent sticking. Add nuts during the last 5 minutes of cooking. Pour boiling hot into hot, sterilized jars, leaving ½-inch headroom, and seal with sterilized lids according to manufacturer's instructions. Process in a boiling-water bath for 10 minutes.

YIELD: About 4 half pints.

Dorothy Watts
Rantoul, Illinois
Greater Champaign
County Fair

Red Currant Jelly

4 pounds (3 quarts) fully ripe red currants
1 cup water
7 cups sugar
1 pouch (3 ounces) liquid fruit pectin

Sterilize canning jars and lids according to directions on page 5.

Place the currants in a large pot and crush them. Add the water and bring to a boil. Simmer, covered, for 10 minutes. Strain through a jelly bag. Measure 5 cups of juice into a large pot. Add sugar and mix well. Bring to a boil over high heat, stirring constantly. Stir in pectin and return to a full rolling boil. Boil hard for 1 minute, stirring constantly. Remove from heat and skim off foam with a metal spoon. Pour at once into sterilized jars, leaving ½-inch headroom, and seal with sterilized lids according to manufacturer's instructions.

YIELD: 8 half pints.

Jeanne Kinney
Marston Mills,
Massachusetts
Barnstable
County Fair

Fig Jam

Another first-place winner for Mrs. D.A. Robichoux, who enters fairs in Louisiana. She cautions that only the very ripest figs will do.

3 pounds very ripe figs
½ cup baking soda
6 quarts boiling water
1 cup cold water
3 cups sugar

Sterilize canning jars and lids according to directions on page 5.

Remove stems from figs, place figs in a large bowl, and sprinkle with baking soda. Cover with boiling water and let stand for 5 minutes. Drain off baking soda solution and rinse figs thoroughly in fresh cold water. In a large pot, crush figs and the 1 cup cold water. Bring slowly to a boil; add the sugar as soon as water boils. Continue cooking rapidly until syrup sheets from the spoon as described in the jelly test, page 6. Stir gently, but frequently, to keep the mixture from scorching. When it reaches the jelly stage, remove from fire and let set for 3 to 5 minutes, stirring gently at regular intervals to dissolve the froth and foam. Pour into sterilized jars, leaving ½-inch headroom, and seal with sterilized lids according to manufacturer's instructions. Process in a hot-water bath (simmer) for 15 minutes.

YIELD: About 3 pints.

Mrs. D.A.
Robichoux
Alexandria,
Louisiana
Rapides Parish Fair
Louisiana State Fair

Fig Preserves

If you are lucky enough to have access to quantities of fresh figs, here is a delicious way to preserve them for the winter.

6 quarts fresh figs
½ cup baking soda
6 quarts boiling water
6 pounds sugar
4 quarts cold water

Select firm, sound figs, discarding all overripe or broken fruit, and place them in a large bowl. Sprinkle figs with baking soda, then cover with boiling water. Let stand for 10 minutes. Pour off soda solution and rinse figs in clear cold water. Let figs drain while you prepare the syrup.

In a large pot, combine sugar and 4 quarts cold water. Boil for 10 minutes, or until sugar dissolves. Add figs to syrup a few at a time, so as not to cool the syrup too much. Boil rapidly for 10 to 15 minutes, or until figs are clear and tender. When the figs are transparent, remove with a slotted spoon and place in one layer in shallow pan(s). Continue boiling the syrup until it is the consistency of honey. Pour the syrup over figs, being sure all figs are covered. Cover with plastic wrap and let stand for 12 to 24 hours.

Sterilize canning jars and lids according to directions on page 5.

Place figs in sterilized jars, leaving ½-inch headspace, and seal with canning lids according to manufacturer's instructions. Process in a hot-water bath (simmer) for 25 minutes.

YIELD: 10 to 12 pints.

Note: If you prefer, you may peel the figs before preserving them. Omit baking soda solution and drop peeled figs directly into boiling sugar syrup.

Mrs. D.A. Robichoux
Alexandria, Louisiana
Rapides Parish Fair
Louisiana State Fair

Grape Jelly

1 container (12 ounces) frozen grape juice concentrate, thawed
1 package ($1\frac{3}{4}$ ounces) powdered fruit pectin
7 cups sugar

Sterilize canning jars and lids according to directions on page 5.

Add enough water to the grape concentrate to make 5 cups. Combine grape juice with pectin in a large saucepan. Bring to a full boil over high heat. Add sugar all at once and return to a full rolling boil, stirring continuously. Boil for 1 minute, stirring constantly. Remove from heat and skim off foam with a metal spoon. Pour into sterilized jars, leaving ½-inch headroom, and seal with sterilized lids according to manufacturer's instructions.

YIELD: About 8 half pints.

Jerry L. Franks
Mount Airy,
North Carolina
Surry County Fair
Dixie Classic Fair

White Grape Jelly

3½ pounds white grapes
1 cup water
¼ cup lemon juice
1 package (1¾ ounces) powdered fruit pectin
5 cups sugar

Wash the grapes and remove stems. Grind them or chop in a food processor. Combine with water and lemon juice in a large saucepan and cook slowly for about 15 minutes. Strain through a jelly bag.

Sterilize canning jars and lids according to directions on page 5.

Combine grape juice and pectin in a saucepan. Bring to a boil over high heat, stirring constantly. Add sugar all at once and return to a full rolling boil, stirring continuously. Boil for 2 minutes, stirring constantly. Remove from heat and skim off foam with a metal spoon. Pour into sterilized jars, leaving ½-inch headroom, and seal with sterilized lids according to manufacturer's instructions.

YIELD: About 7 half pints.

Myron Pestana
Patterson, California
Stanislaus
County Fair

Honeydew Chutney

1 large honeydew melon
¼ cup pickling salt
2 cups cider vinegar
½ teaspoon salt
2 cups light brown sugar
1 teaspoon ground ginger
¼ teaspoon red pepper flakes
¼ teaspoon coarsely crushed whole allspice
1 piece of cinnamon, about 2 inches long
1 cup chopped onion
½ cup chopped green bell pepper
½ cup chopped red bell pepper
1 garlic clove, finely chopped
½ cup dried currants
⅓ cup brandy or cognac

Remove seeds from melon and cut flesh into 1-inch cubes (about 8 cups). Place cubes in a large bowl, add cold water to cover, and stir in ¼ cup salt. Refrigerate, covered, overnight. Drain the melon and rinse in cold water.

Sterilize canning jars and lids according to directions on page 5.

Place all ingredients except currants and brandy into a large saucepan. Heat to boiling, stirring constantly. Add currants and brandy. Simmer uncovered until thick, about 2 hours. It will reduce to about half the volume. Stir frequently.

Pour into sterilized jars, leaving ½-inch headroom, and seal with sterilized lids according to manufacturer's instructions. Process in a boiling-water bath for 10 minutes.

YIELD: About 4 half pints.

Sonia Anderson
Alameda,
California
California
State Fair

Huckleberry Jelly

An original recipe from Betty Jones that has won her a blue ribbon five times in a row!

1 gallon huckleberries (to make 4 cups juice)
1 package (1¾ ounces) powdered fruit pectin
6 cups sugar

Crush the berries or cook them briefly and strain through a jelly bag to get 4 cups of juice.

Sterilize canning jars and lids according to directions on page 5.

Combine juice and pectin in a large saucepan and bring to a boil, stirring frequently. Add sugar and return to a full rolling boil, stirring constantly. Boil for 1 minute, stirring continuously. Remove from heat and skim off foam with a metal spoon. Pour into sterilized jars, leaving ½-inch headroom, and seal with sterilized lids according to manufacturer's instructions.

YIELD: About 6 half pints.

Betty L. Jones
Kalispell, Montana
Northwest
Montana Fair

Kiwi Marmalade

Mrs. Perry Coy averages fifty to seventy entries every year in the preserved foods division of the Fresno Fair. Her Kiwi Marmalade is an original recipe and a great family favorite.

1 orange
2 lemons
1 cup water
1 pound kiwis
7 cups sugar
1 pouch (3 ounces) liquid fruit pectin

Sterilize canning jars and lids according to directions on page 5.

Cut the orange and one of the lemons into quarter sections; discard the seeds. Slice the fruit wafer thin. Squeeze juice from remaining lemon and measure 2 tablespoons of juice. Combine fruit, juice, and water in a saucepan. Cover and simmer 20 minutes, stirring occasionally.

Peel the kiwis and purée them in a food processor or blender. Combine kiwi purée with orange and lemon mixture. You should have about 4½ cups of prepared fruit. Stir in sugar and bring to a full rolling boil. Boil hard for 1 minute, stirring occasionally. Remove from heat and immediately stir in pectin. Skim off any foam with a large metal spoon. Pour into sterilized jars, leaving ½-inch headroom, and seal with sterilized lids according to manufacturer's instructions. Process in a boiling-water bath for 10 minutes. Let marmalade mellow for 3 weeks before using.

YIELD: 7 or 8 half pints.

Mrs. Perry Coy
Clovis, California
Fresno Fair

Kumquat Marmalade

3 cups marmalade stock
2¼ cups sugar

To make marmalade stock: Select about 4 cups of kumquats. Wash, slice crosswise into thin sections, and remove seeds; or, cut in halves, remove seeds, and put through a food chopper. Measure the prepared fruit and place in a saucepan. For each cup of fruit, add 3 cups of water. Bring to a boil. Cook about 15 minutes. Allow to stand overnight.

When you are ready to make marmalade, sterilize canning jars and lids according to directions on page 5.

Measure 3 cups of marmalade stock. Put in a large saucepan and bring to a boil. Add sugar and cook rapidly to 220°F on candy or jelly thermometer. Remove from heat and cool to 190°F. Stir well to redistribute fruit. Pour into sterilized jars, leaving ½-inch headroom, and seal with sterilized lids according to manufacturer's instructions. Process in a boiling-water bath for 10 minutes.

YIELD: About 4 half pints.

Mrs. Geraldean Roy
Fort Pierce, Florida
St. Lucie County Fair

Mint Jelly

1½ cups firmly packed fresh mint leaves
2¼ cups water
2 tablespoons lemon juice
1 or 2 drops green food coloring
3½ cups sugar
1 pouch (3 ounces) liquid fruit pectin

Sterilize canning jars and lids according to directions on page 5.

Rinse the mint leaves, place in a large saucepan, and crush. Add the water and bring quickly to a boil. Remove from heat, cover, and let stand for 10 minutes.

Strain to remove the mint leaves and measure 1¾ cups of mint extract. Add lemon juice and food coloring to the mint extract. Put in a saucepan with the sugar and mix well. Bring to a boil over high heat, stirring constantly. Immediately stir in the pectin. Return to a full rolling boil and boil hard for 1 minute, stirring constantly. Remove from heat and skim off foam with a large metal spoon. Pour into sterilized jars, leaving ½-inch headroom, and seal with sterilized lids according to manufacturer's instructions.

YIELD: 3 to 4 half pints.

Jeanne Kinney
Marston Mills,
Massachusetts
Barnstable
County Fair

Mixed Fruit Preserves

Any combination of the following fruit:
peaches, papayas, mangoes, pears
1 cup pineapple juice
¼ cup lemon juice
7½ cups sugar
2 kiwis, peeled and sliced
1 pouch (3 ounces) liquid fruit pectin

Sterilize canning jars and lids according to directions on page 5.

Choose your fruit. Peel and remove pits. Chop the fruits in any combination to measure 4 cups. Combine fruit with pineapple juice, lemon juice, and sugar in a large saucepan. Bring to a full rolling boil. Add kiwi slices, return to a boil, and boil hard for 1 minute, stirring constantly. Remove from heat and add pectin. Stir for several minutes and skim off foam with a metal spoon. Pour into hot, sterilized jars, leaving ½-inch headroom, and seal with sterilized lids according to manufacturer's instructions. Process in a boiling-water bath for 10 minutes.

YIELD: About 8 half pints.

Anne Marie Kocias
Strongsville, Ohio
Cuyahoga
County Fair

Orange-Pineapple Marmalade

Myron Pestana has always been interested in cooking, and after retirement wanted a hobby. He and his wife grow most of their own fruits and vegetables and keep busy making prizewinning pickles and preserves.

3 medium-ripe oranges, preferably Valencias or Sevilles
4 cups water
2 cups crushed pineapple, unsweetened
1 package (1¾ ounces) powdered fruit pectin
6 cups sugar

Sterilize canning jars and lids according to directions on page 5.

Wash oranges and use a small, very sharp knife to cut away the thin, outer layer of orange rind. Slice rind into small pieces and preserve. Peel away the remaining white pith and discard. Cut peeled oranges into small pieces. Combine orange pieces, orange peel, and water in a saucepan and simmer slowly, stirring frequently, until orange peel is tender. Remove any seeds as you stir. A little water may be added, if necessary, to make 2 full cups of orange and peel.

Mix in crushed pineapple. Bring to a boil, add pectin, then sugar, stirring continuously. Bring to a rolling boil, continuing to stir, and boil 4 minutes. Pour into hot, sterilized jars, leaving ½-inch headroom, and seal with sterilized lids according to manufacturer's instructions. Process in a boiling-water bath for 10 minutes.

YIELD: 7 or 8 half pints.

Myron Pestana
Patterson, California
Stanislaus County Fair

Perfect Peach Preserves

4 cups sliced or quartered peaches
4 cups sugar
1 package (1¾ ounces) powdered fruit pectin

Sterilize canning jars and lids according to directions on page 5.

Mix peaches with sugar and let stand, stirring frequently, until sugar has dissolved. Bring peach mixture to a boil and cook, stirring frequently, for 15 minutes. Add pectin and boil for 12 to 15 minutes longer. Remove from heat and skim foam from top of mixture. Pour into sterilized jars, leaving ½-inch headroom, and seal with sterilized lids according to manufacturer's instructions. Process in a boiling-water bath for 10 minutes.

YIELD: 6 to 7 half pints.

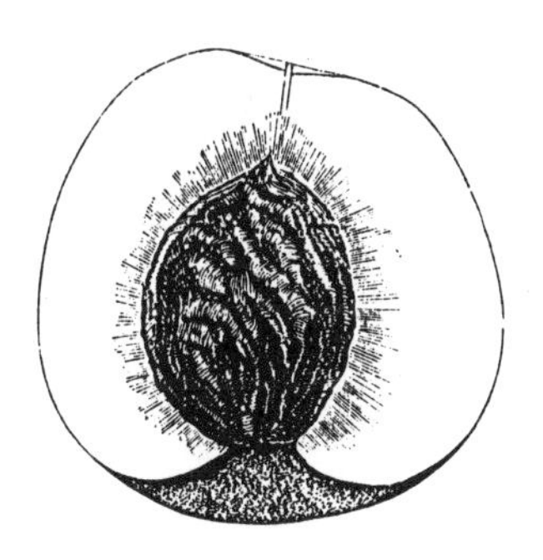

Mrs. Vae Lambeth
Winston-Salem, North Carolina
Dixie Classic Fair

Peach Jam

3 pounds fully ripe peaches
2 tablespoons lemon juice
1 package (1¾ ounces) powdered fruit pectin
5½ cups sugar

Sterilize canning jars and lids according to directions on page 5.

To peel peaches, dip in scalding hot water and then into cold water: skins will slip right off. Remove the pits. Slice peaches into small pieces and crush with your hands.

Combine peaches with lemon juice and pectin in a large saucepan. Bring to a full boil. Add sugar all at once and return to a full rolling boil, stirring constantly. Boil for 1 minute, stirring. Remove from heat and skim off foam with a metal spoon. Pour into sterilized jars, leaving ½-inch headroom, and seal with sterilized lids according to manufacturer's instructions. Process in a boiling-water bath for 10 minutes.

YIELD: About 7 half pints.

Jerry L. Franks
Mount Airy,
North Carolina
Surry County Fair
Dixie Classic Fair

Peach Marmalade

This peach marmalade has won first place at both the Rapides Parish Fair and the Louisiana State Fair for eighty-year-old Mrs. Robichoux. The marmalade contains small uniform pieces of fruit, large enough to be seen. The jelly is clear and translucent.

½ pound sugar
1 cup water or peach juice
2 pounds thinly sliced peaches (about 6 cups)

Sterilize canning jars and lids according to directions on page 5.

Dissolve half the sugar in water or juice over moderate heat. Add the sliced peaches and boil slowly until tender. Add the remaining sugar and boil rapidly until syrup sheets from the spoon as described in the jelly test, page 6. Cool 3 to 5 minutes. Place in canning jars, leaving ½-inch headspace, and seal with canning lids according to manufacturer's instructions. Process 15 minutes in a hot-water bath (simmer).

YIELD: About 6 half pints.

Mrs. D.A. Robichoux
Alexandria, Louisiana
Rapides Parish Fair
Louisiana State Fair

Rosy Melba Peach Jam

1½ pounds ripe peaches
¼ cup lemon juice
2 cups red raspberries
7 cups sugar
2 pouches (6 ounces) liquid pectin
1 teaspoon almond extract

Sterilize canning jars and lids according to directions on page 5.

Peel, pit, and crush peaches. Measure 2 cups peach pulp into a bowl. Add 2 tablespoons lemon juice. Stir gently and let stand. In another bowl, crush berries and add remaining lemon juice. Stir well. Combine peaches, berries, and sugar in a heavy pot. Mix well and bring to a full rolling boil. Boil for 1 minute, stirring constantly. Remove from heat and add pectin. Stir and skim for several minutes. Add almond extract. Pour into sterilized jars, leaving ½-inch headroom, and seal with sterilized lids according to manufacturer's instructions. Process in a boiling-water bath for 10 minutes.

YIELD: 8 half pints.

Patricia McManus
Wallingford,
Connecticut
Durham Fair

Peach Melba Conserve

½ cup slivered almonds
4 cups peeled, sliced peaches
1 cup raspberries
3 tablespoons lemon juice
1 teaspoon grated lemon peel
1 package (1¾ ounces) powdered fruit pectin
6 cups sugar

Sterilize canning jars and lids according to directions on page 5.

Toast almonds in a heavy skillet over high heat, stirring constantly. Reserve. In a large saucepan, combine peaches, raspberries, lemon juice, grated lemon peel, and pectin. Bring to a hard boil while stirring. Add sugar, stir, and bring to a full, rolling boil. Boil for 1 minute, stirring. Remove from heat and stir and skim for 5 minutes to keep fruit from floating. Stir in almonds. Pour into sterilized jars, leaving ½-inch headroom, and seal with sterilized lids according to manufacturer's instructions. Process in a boiling-water bath for 10 minutes.

YIELD: 6 or 7 half pints.

Sonia Anderson
Alameda, California
California State Fair

Pear Preserves

12 cups peeled, cored, and sliced pears
9 cups sugar
½ lemon, sliced thin

Cover the pear slices with sugar and let stand overnight. Enough liquid will be produced to allow cooking without adding water.

Sterilize canning jars and lids according to directions on page 5.

Stir to mix pears, sugar, and juice. Add the lemon slices. Bring to a simmer and cook over low heat, stirring frequently, until pears are tender, clear, and caramel colored and liquid is consistency of honey. Cooking time will be 1½ to 2 hours. Pour preserves into sterilized jars, leaving ½-inch headroom, and seal with sterilized lids according to manufacturer's instructions. Process in a boiling-water bath for 10 minutes.

YIELD: 8 to 10 half pints.

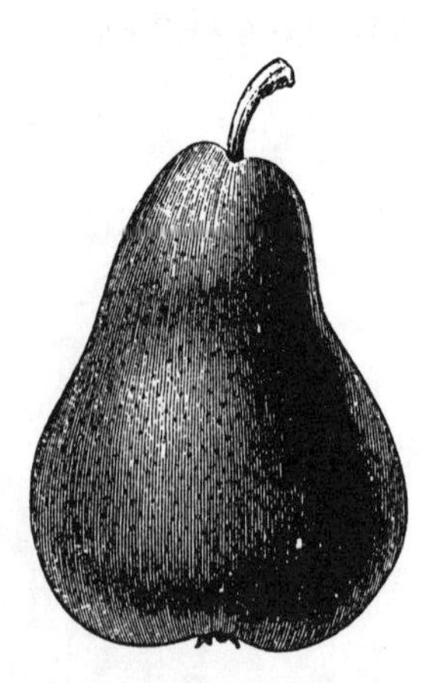

Nell Starling
Garland, Texas
State Fair of Texas

Pear Butter

15 to 20 medium-size pears
3 cups sugar
1 cup light brown sugar
½ teaspoon kosher salt
¼ cup fresh lemon juice
½ teaspoon nutmeg
½ teaspoon allspice
1½ cups apple cider
½ teaspoon almond extract (optional)

Sterilize canning jars and lids according to directions on page 5.

Pare, core, and cut pears into small pieces. Place fruit in a blender or food processor and blend until smooth. You should have about 2 quarts of pear pulp. Combine pulp and remaining ingredients in a large metal kettle. Cook gently over medium heat until mixture becomes thick, about 1 hour. Pour into sterilized jars, leaving ½-inch headroom, and seal with sterilized lids according to manufacturer's instructions. Process in a boiling-water bath for 10 minutes. Store in a cool dry place for at least 2 weeks before serving.

YIELD: About 3 pints.

Ardelle Laurence
Tarzana, California
Los Angeles
County Fair

Pear Tomato Chutney

15 large red ripe tomatoes
6 pears
1 large or 2 small cucumbers
2 to 3 medium-size onions
3 red bell peppers
1 cup seedless raisins
3 cups brown sugar (packed)
3 cups white vinegar
1 hot red pepper
1 garlic clove, crushed
1 tablespoon ground ginger
1 teaspoon ground cinnamon
1 teaspoon salt

Sterilize canning jars and lids according to directions on page 5.

Peel, core, and chop the tomatoes. Peel, core, and chop the pears. Peel, seed, and chop cucumbers. Peel onions and slice into thin rings. Core and chop the peppers.

Combine all the ingredients in a large pot. Cook slowly until thick, approximately 2 hours. Stir frequently to prevent sticking. When chutney is thick, remove from heat. Pour into sterilized jars, leaving ½-inch headroom, and seal with sterilized lids according to manufacturer's instructions. Process in a boiling-water bath for 10 minutes.

YIELD: About 3 pints.

Opal Reed
Tyler, Texas
Smith County Fair

Pepper Jelly

1 cup finely chopped green bell pepper
1 cup finely chopped red bell pepper
¼ cup finely chopped jalapeño pepper
6½ cups sugar
1½ cups cider vinegar
2 pouches (6 ounces) liquid fruit pectin

Sterilize canning jars and lids according to directions on page 5.

Combine peppers, sugar, and vinegar in a large saucepan and bring to a boil. Immediately stir in liquid pectin, bring to a full, rolling boil, and boil for 1 minute, stirring constantly. Pour into hot, sterilized jars, leaving ½-inch headroom, and seal with sterilized lids according to manufacturer's instructions.

YIELD: About 8 half pints.

Sharon Sullens Poe
Norman,
Oklahoma
State Fair
of Oklahoma

Jalapeño Pepper Jelly

Serve this sweet spicy jelly spread on cream cheese over a cracker, suggests Linda Strong, who got her prizewinning recipe from friends. One word of caution: These peppers are hot, hot, hot, so wear rubber gloves if your skin is sensitive.

6 fresh jalapeño peppers, seeded and sliced
¼ cup water
6⅔ cups sugar
2 cups cider vinegar
2 pouches (6 ounces) liquid fruit pectin
1 or 2 drops green food coloring

Sterilize canning jars and lids according to directions on page 5.

Combine peppers with water in the bowl of a food processor or blender. Process to a fine pulp. In a large saucepan, combine pepper mixture, sugar, and vinegar. Bring to a boil and boil 4 minutes. Remove from heat and add pectin and food coloring. Stir well. Pour into sterilized jars, leaving ½-inch headroom, and seal with sterilized lids according to manufacturer's instructions.

YIELD: 8 half pints.

Linda Strong
Lindale, Texas
East Texas Fair

Wild Plum Preserves

"I obtained this recipe from Mrs. Sid Houghton of Erwin, South Dakota, the fall of 1948," writes Irene Kverne. "Mrs. Houghton came to my rescue early in my married life the year we had a bumper crop of wild plums. She was an elderly lady at the time and has long since left this world, but every fall when I make up our supply of plum preserves I think of her and her kindness. Absolutely no preservative is included and nothing is needed to make it jell." This recipe has repeatedly won a blue ribbon at the Central States Fair.

Plums
Water
Sugar

Sterilize canning jars and lids according to directions on page 5.

Wash plums and place them in a large saucepan. Cover with water and bring to a boil. Cook plums until very tender, stirring frequently. Drain plums but save the juice for making jelly later.

Pit the plums and measure the remaining pulp. For each 1 cup of pulp, add 1 cup water and 2 cups sugar. Boil fairly fast until nice and thick. This usually takes about 1 hour.

Pour into hot, sterilized jars, leaving ½-inch headroom, and seal with sterilized lids according to manufacturer's instructions. Process in a boiling-water bath for 10 minutes.

YIELD: 1 cup pulp will yield 1 half pint.

Irene Kverne
Rapid City,
South Dakota
Central States Fair

Quince Jelly

Quinces
Water
Sugar

Sterilize canning jars and lids according to directions on page 5.

Cut quinces into small pieces. Cover with water and cook until tender. Strain through a jelly bag. Measure the juice and bring to a boil. Add 1 cup sugar for each 1 cup juice. Boil rapidly until syrup sheets from the spoon as described in the jelly test, page 6. Pour into hot, sterilized jars, leaving ½-inch headroom, and seal with sterilized lids according to manufacturer's instructions.

YIELD: Each cup of juice will yield 1 half pint.

Mrs. D.A. Robichoux
Alexandria, Louisiana
Rapides Parish Fair
Louisiana State Fair

Red Raspberry Jam

4 pounds red raspberries
¼ cup lemon juice
½ package powdered fruit pectin
7½ cups sugar

Sterilize canning jars and lids according to directions on page 5.

Crush raspberries, a few at a time, to make sure all are crushed. Place crushed raspberries into a large pot. Add lemon and pectin and stir well. Over high heat, bring to a rolling boil. Add sugar and return to a full rolling boil, stirring constantly. Boil exactly 4 minutes, stirring continuously. Remove from heat and skim off foam with a metal spoon. Pour into sterilized jars, leaving ½-inch headroom, and seal with sterilized lids according to manufacturer's instructions. Process in a boiling-water bath for 10 minutes.

YIELD: 8 half pints.

Nancylee Hartmann
San Jose, California
Santa Clara
County Fair

Wild Raspberry Jelly

2½ quarts fresh wild raspberries (for 4 cups juice)
1 package (1¾ ounces) powdered fruit pectin
5½ cups sugar

Crush the berries one layer at a time and strain through a jelly bag, to make 4 cups juice.

Sterilize canning jars and lids according to directions on page 5.

Combine raspberry juice with pectin in a large saucepan and bring to a boil, stirring frequently. Boil for 1 minute. Add the sugar and return to a full rolling boil, stirring constantly. Boil hard for 1 minute, stirring continuously. Remove from heat and skim off foam with a metal spoon. Pour into sterilized jars, leaving ½-inch headroom, and seal with sterilized lids according to manufacturer's instructions.

YIELD: About 6 half pints.

Karen Jaramillo
Springville, Arizona
Apache County Fair
Arizona State Fair

Wild Raspberry Jam

5 cups fresh wild raspberries (you may use frozen berries)
1 package (1¾ ounces) powdered fruit pectin
7 cups sugar

Sterilize canning jars and lids according to directions on page 5.

Place berries in a large pot, but do not crush them. This will keep the pulp and seeds from separating. Add pectin and bring to a boil. Let boil 2 minutes, then add sugar. Stir well and return to a full rolling boil, stirring constantly. Boil for 2 minutes, stirring continuously. Remove from heat and skim off foam with a metal spoon. Pour into sterilized jars, leaving ½-inch headroom, and seal with sterilized lids according to manufacturer's instructions. Process in a boiling-water bath for 10 minutes.

YIELD: 8 to 10 half pints.

Karen Jaramillo
Springville, Arizona
Apache County Fair
Arizona State Fair

Rhubarb Jam

This is a family recipe handed down from Alice Thiele's grandmother. It is unusual in that it calls for no water at all. It has won ribbons at the Sioux Empire Fair and the Minnehaha County Fair.

5 cups washed and chopped rhubarb
3 cups sugar
1 package (3 ounces) strawberry or raspberry Jell-O

Sterilize canning jars and lids according to directions on page 5.

Put rhubarb in a large heavy pot and let it come to a boil over low heat. Add sugar and stir until dissolved. Let boil 15 minutes and remove from heat. Add Jell-O and stir until dissolved. Pour into sterilized jars, leaving ½-inch headroom, and seal with sterilized lids according to manufacturer's instructions. Process in a boiling-water bath for 10 minutes.

Alternatively, pour jam into airtight containers and freeze.

YIELD: 3 to 4 half pints.

Alice P. Thiele
Brandon, South Dakota
Sioux Empire Fair
Minnehaha County Fair

Farm-Fresh Strawberry Jam

Anne Marie Kocias, a fourth-grade teacher, writes that she uses a standard recipe for her strawberry jam with one very important difference. "I pick my berries between 8:30 and 9:30 A.M., as early in the morning as I possibly can. I make jam *as soon as* I walk in the door." Her strawberries are picked at Rado's Farm in North Olmstead, Ohio. Make this jam within two hours of picking your strawberries.

2 quarts freshly picked strawberries
1 package (1¾ ounces) powdered fruit pectin
3 cups sugar

Sterilize canning jars and lids according to directions on page 5.

Wash the strawberries, removing stems and hulls. Crush berries one layer at a time. Measure 4 cups of crushed berries into a large saucepan and combine with pectin and sugar. Bring to a full rolling boil over high heat. Boil hard, stirring constantly, for 1 minute. Remove from heat and skim off foam with a metal spoon. Pour into sterilized jars, leaving ½-inch headroom, and seal with sterilized lids according to manufacturer's instructions. Process in a boiling-water bath for 5 minutes.

YIELD: 8 half pints.

Anne Marie Kocias
Strongsville, Ohio
Cuyahoga
County Fair

Strawberry Preserves

Grandmother's recipe won Nancylee Hartmann the honor of Best in Division at the Santa Clara County Fair.

2 quarts medium-size strawberries
5 cups sugar
½ cup lemon juice

Remove stems and caps from strawberries and wash them. Put strawberries in a 2-quart pot and add just enough water so you can see the water through the strawberries (about ¼ cup). Add sugar and lemon juice. Bring to a boil slowly. Boil for 15 minutes. Pour into a glass baking dish. As strawberries cool, stir with a wooden spoon. Let stand overnight.

Sterilize canning jars and lids according to directions on page 5.

Pour strawberries into sterilized jars, leaving ½-inch headroom, and seal with sterilized lids according to manufacturer's instructions. Process in a boiling-water bath for 15 minutes, exactly.

YIELD: About 4 half pints.

Nancylee Hartmann
San Jose, California
Santa Clara
County Fair

Strawberry Jelly

2½ quarts strawberries
1 package (1¾ ounces) powdered fruit pectin
5 cups sugar

Sterilize canning jars and lids according to directions on page 5.

Wash the strawberries and remove stems and caps. Crush the berries one layer at a time and strain through a jelly bag. Measure 3½ cups juice. Combine strawberry juice and pectin in a large saucepan. Bring to a boil, stirring constantly. Immediately stir in sugar. Return to a full rolling boil, stirring constantly, and boil for 1 minute, stirring continuously. Remove from heat and skim off foam with a metal spoon. Pour into sterilized jars, leaving ½-inch headroom, and seal with sterilized lids according to manufacturer's instructions.

YIELD: 5 to 6 half pints.

Mrs. J.T. (Helen) Woodruff
Mount Airy, North Carolina
Surry County Agricultural Fair

Strawberry-Rhubarb Jam

2¼ cups chopped rhubarb
½ cup water
2½ cups strawberries
1 package (1¾ ounces) powdered fruit pectin
6 cups sugar

Sterilize canning jars and lids according to directions on page 5.

Combine rhubarb and water in a saucepan and simmer until rhubarb is tender, about 2 minutes. Crush the rhubarb to break up some of the fibers. Sort and wash strawberries, using only fully ripe berries. Remove stems and caps and crush berries.

Combine rhubarb, strawberries, and pectin in a large saucepan and bring to a full boil, stirring frequently. Add sugar all at once and return to a full rolling boil, stirring continuously. Boil, stirring, for 1 minute. Remove from heat and skim off foam with a metal spoon. Pour into sterilized jars, leaving ½-inch headroom, and seal with sterilized lids according to manufacturer's instructions. Process in a boiling-water bath for 10 minutes.

YIELD: About 5 half pints.

Jerry L. Franks
Mount Airy,
North Carolina
Surry County Fair
Dixie Classic Fair

Red Tomato Jam

1 pound ripe tomatoes
1 pound sugar
Grated rind and juice of 1 lemon
1 cinnamon stick

Scald and skin the tomatoes. Cut away the stem end. Place tomatoes in a large bowl and cover with sugar. Let stand for 12 hours.

Sterilize canning jars and lids according to directions on page 5.

Drain the tomatoes and place the juice in a large saucepan. Boil until syrup sheets from the spoon as described in the jelly test, page 6. Add the tomatoes, lemon rind and juice, and cinnamon. Cook until thick. Remove cinnamon stick. Pour into sterilized jars, leaving ½-inch headroom, and seal with sterilized lids according to manufacturer's instructions. Process in a boiling-water bath for 10 minutes.

YIELD: 4 to 6 half pints.

Barbara Carpenter
West Allis, Wisconsin
Wisconsin State Fair

Tomato Preserves

2¼ cups tomato pulp (from fresh ripe tomatoes)
4 tablespoons lemon juice
Grated rind of 1 lemon
⅛ teaspoon salt
¼ cup boiling water
1 package (1¾ ounces) powdered fruit pectin
3½ cups sugar

Sterilize canning jars and lids according to directions on page 5.

In a large saucepan (preferably nonstick), combine tomato pulp, lemon juice, lemon rind, salt, and boiling water. Heat to boiling, add pectin, and bring to a full rolling boil. Add sugar and return to a rolling boil, stirring constantly. Boil for 4 minutes, stirring frequently. Remove from heat and skim froth from the top. Pour into sterilized jars, leaving ½-inch headroom, and seal with sterilized lids according to manufacturer's instructions. Process in a boiling-water bath for 10 minutes.

YIELD: About 5 half pints.

LaVonne Troxell
Fountain Valley,
California
Orange County Fair

Tomato Pineapple Preserves

2 pounds small ripe tomatoes
4 cups sugar
1 can (11 ounces) crushed pineapple and juice
¼ cup lemon juice

Scald and peel the tomatoes. Cut them in half or quarter them, depending on their size. Place in a large bowl and sprinkle with sugar. Stir gently, cover with a towel, and let stand overnight or at least 8 hours.

Sterilize canning jars and lids according to directions on page 5.

Place a sieve over a saucepan and drain tomatoes for 10 to 15 minutes. Add pineapple with juice to the tomato juice. Bring to a boil. Stir occasionally until temperature measures 220°F on a candy or jelly thermometer. Add tomatoes and boil until syrup sheets from the spoon as described in the jelly test, page 6. Pour into sterilized jars, leaving ½-inch headroom, and seal with sterilized lids according to manufacturer's instructions. Process in a boiling-water bath for 10 minutes.

YIELD: 4 half pints.

Sonia Anderson
Alameda, California
California State Fair

Tropical Jam

Opal Reed calls this recipe, "my own concoction," and it has won first place at the Smith County Fair.

1 can (12 ounces) mango nectar
1 can (12 ounces) guava nectar
1 can (6 ounces) frozen tangerine juice, thawed
¾ cup water
1 package (1¾ ounces) powdered fruit pectin
1½ to 2 cups sugar

Sterilize canning jars and lids according to directions on page 5.

Mix all the above ingredients except sugar in a deep saucepan. Bring to a boil. Stir in sugar and bring to a rolling boil. Boil for 3 to 5 minutes. Remove from heat and skim top. Pour into sterilized jars, leaving ½-inch headroom, and seal with sterilized lids according to manufacturer's instructions. Process in a boiling-water bath for 10 minutes.

YIELD: 6 half pints.

Opal M. Reed
Tyler, Texas
Smith County Fair

Wine Jelly

Champagne, rośe, or other full-bodied white wines make lovely jellies. For a red jelly, choose a fortified wine such as port, madeira, or sherry. Other red wines seems to be too acidic to make good jelly.

4½ cups sugar
1 package (1¾ ounces) powdered fruit pectin
¾ cup water
3 cups wine

Sterilize canning jars and lids according to directions on page 5.

Measure sugar and set aside. Mix pectin and water in a large saucepan. Bring to a boil over high heat. Boil 1 minute, stirring constantly. Immediately add wine and sugar and cook, stirring, over medium heat, keeping the mixture at just below the boiling point. Cook, stirring, until the sugar is dissolved, about 5 minutes. Remove from heat and skim if necessary. Pour into sterilized jars, leaving ½-inch headroom, and seal with sterilized lids according to manufacturer's instructions.

YIELD: 4 to 5 half pints.

Marjorie Sperling
Walbach, Nebraska
Howard County Fair

Zucchini-Pineapple-Apricot Jam

This family recipe from Jennette Smith is a delicious way to use up a bumper crop of zucchini.

6 cups peeled and grated zucchini (remove seeds from large zucchini; in small ones the seeds are unformed)
½ cup lemon juice
1 cup drained crushed pineapple
1 package (1¾ ounces) powdered fruit pectin
6 cups sugar
1 package (6 ounces) apricot Jell-O

Sterilize canning jars and lids according to directions on page 5.

Combine zucchini and lemon juice in a saucepan. Mix and cook for 1 hour over low heat, stirring occasionally. Add pineapple, pectin, and sugar. Bring to a boil and boil for 6 minutes. Add Jell-O and stir well. Pour into sterilized jars, leaving ½-inch headroom, and seal with sterilized lids according to manufacturer's instructions. Process in a boiling-water bath for 10 minutes.

YIELD: About 8 half pints.

Jennette Smith
Turlock, California
Stanislaus
County Fair

Resources

Readers who are interested in regional or specialty cookbooks may purchase them by mail from the following organizations:

Blue Ribbon Baked Goods
Anchorage Fur Rendezvous
P.O. Box 773
Anchorage, Alaska 99510

Award Winning Recipes
L.A. County Fair
P.O. Box 2250
Pomona, California 91769

Prize Winners Plus Cookbook
State Fair of Oklahoma
P.O. Box 74943
Oklahoma City, Oklahoma 73147

Prize Winning Recipes
State Fair of Texas
P.O. Box 26010
Dallas, Texas 75226

Savor It!
Michigan 4-H Foundation
1407 South Harrison Avenue
East Lansing, Michigan 48823

Index

D

E

F

G

Q

R

S